BEYOND THE KNOWN

EXPLORING THE FRONTIERS OF
PARAPSYCHOLOGY

ELLIOTT MIDDLETON PHD

The universe is full of magical things patiently waiting for our wits to grow sharper.

— EDEN PHILLPOTTS

FOREWORD

In a world increasingly defined by scientific precision, the exploration of parapsychology offers a compelling challenge to our conventional understanding of reality. This book stands at the crossroads of science and the unknown, daring to ask questions that stretch the limits of empirical inquiry. As a researcher, I have always valued the courage it takes to explore these frontiers, where the lines between the physical and the metaphysical blur and consciousness itself seems to hold untapped potential.

I have meticulously crafted a narrative that explores telepathy, psychokinesis, and remote viewing and delves into the philosophical and scientific implications of these enigmatic experiences. Through rigorous analysis and thoughtful reflection, this book challenges the reader to consider the possibility that our understanding of consciousness is still in its infancy.

What makes this work particularly valuable is its balanced approach—neither dismissing skepticism nor succumbing to unfounded speculation. This careful balance, rooted in rigorous research and critical thinking, elevates the discourse on parapsychology and provides a solid foundation for future research.

As we venture into the depths of this exploration, I encourage readers to maintain an open mind and a critical eye. The questions raised here are not merely academic; they strike at the core of what it means to be human and conscious and engage with a universe that may be far more mysterious than we have imagined.

Elliott Middleton, PhD

August, 2024

1

THE BIRTH OF SPIRITUALISM AND EARLY PSYCHIC PHENOMENA

1.1 Definition and Scope of Parapsychology

Parapsychology is the scientific study of phenomena that lie beyond the scope of traditional psychology and the natural sciences. These phenomena, often referred to as psi, include experiences such as telepathy (mind-to-mind communication), psychokinesis (mind over matter), clairvoyance (remote viewing), and precognition (foreknowledge of future events). The term "parapsychology" was first coined in the late 19th century by German philosopher Max Dessoir, and it gained broader recognition in the early 20th century as researchers began systematically investigating these unusual experiences.

While often regarded with skepticism, parapsychology has a long and rich history of serious inquiry. Researchers in this field are not merely interested in documenting strange occurrences; they aim to understand the mechanisms underlying psi phenomena, test their replicability under controlled conditions, and explore their implications for our understanding of consciousness and reality. Parapsychology is interdisciplinary, drawing on methods and theories from psychology, physics, neuroscience, and philosophy.

One of the primary challenges in defining parapsychology is its controversial status within the scientific community. Unlike more established fields of study, parapsychology often faces the dual challenge of being seen as both a legitimate scientific endeavor and a realm of pseudoscience. This tension is partly due to the difficulty in reproducing psi phenomena consistently and the lack of a universally accepted theoretical framework that explains these phenomena in terms of established scientific principles.

In addition to telepathy, psychokinesis, clairvoyance, and precognition, parapsychology also investigates other phenomena that challenge our conventional understanding of the mind and reality. These include out-of-body experiences, near-death experiences, and mediumship (the purported ability to communicate with the dead). Each of these phenomena raises profound questions about the nature of consciousness, the relationship between mind and body, and the possibility of life after death.

The scope of parapsychology extends beyond the mere collection of anecdotal reports. Researchers in this field employ rigorous methodologies, including controlled experiments, statistical analysis, and meta-analysis, to evaluate the validity of psi phenomena. For instance, the Ganzfeld experiment, a well-known method in parapsychology, involves placing participants in a sensory-deprived environment to test for telepathic abilities. Similarly, random number generator experiments have been used to study psychokinesis, while remote viewing protocols have been developed to test clairvoyance under controlled conditions.

As parapsychology continues to evolve, it remains a field that challenges our deepest assumptions about reality and the limits of human potential. Whether psi phenomena prove genuine or not, exploring them invites us to question what we know about the mind, consciousness, and the nature of the universe.

1.2 Historical Background

The history of parapsychology is rich and complex, tracing back to ancient times when phenomena like telepathy and precognition were often interpreted through religious or mystical lenses. In many cultures, these experiences were associated with shamans, priests, or oracles believed to have unique access to otherworldly knowledge. Ancient texts from Egypt, Greece, and India reference what we now consider psi phenomena, indicating that human fascination with these experiences is not modern.

However, the formal scientific investigation of psi phenomena began in the late 19th century, during a period of burgeoning interest in the occult and spiritualism. The rise of spiritualism, which claimed to communicate with the dead through mediums, sparked widespread curiosity and skepticism. This movement led to the establishment of societies dedicated to studying psychic phenomena, most notably the Society for Psychical Research (SPR) in London, founded in 1882. The SPR's mission was to investigate paranormal claims using scientific methods, and it brought together prominent figures from various fields, including psychology, physics, and philosophy.

The work of researchers like Frederic W. H. Myers, one of the founders of the SPR, laid the groundwork for parapsychology as a distinct field of study. Myers's book *Human Personality and Its Survival of Bodily Death* (1903) is considered a seminal work in parapsychology, exploring topics such as telepathy, hypnotism, and survival after death. Myers and his contemporaries sought to apply rigorous scientific methods to studying these phenomena to separate genuine psychic experiences from fraud and superstition.

In the early 20th century, parapsychology gained further legitimacy through the work of American psychologist J. B. Rhine, often regarded as the father of modern parapsychology. At Duke University, Rhine and his colleagues conducted systematic experiments on telepathy, clairvoyance, and psychokinesis, using statistical methods to evaluate their findings. Rhine's experiments, particularly those involving Zener cards, were groundbreaking in their attempt to quantify psi phenomena and demonstrate their existence under controlled conditions. Rhine's work led to the establishment of the Parapsychology Laboratory at Duke, which became a center for research in the field.

Despite these early advances, parapsychology has always been a field fraught with controversy. The inability to consistently reproduce psi phenomena in laboratory settings has been a major stumbling block, leading many in the scientific community to remain skeptical of parapsychologists' claims. Additionally, the field has often been associated with pseudoscience, partly due to the sensational claims made by some individuals outside the scientific community and the occasional cases of fraud that have marred its reputation.

Nevertheless, the history of parapsychology is also a history of perseverance and innovation. Researchers have continued developing new methodologies, technologies, and theoretical frameworks to understand psi phenomena. For example, the development of the Ganzfeld procedure in the 1970s provided a new way to test telepathy by reducing sensory input and isolating the mind's potential to receive information from distant sources. Similarly, advancements in quantum physics have led some researchers to explore the possibility that non-local interactions at the quantum level might explain psi phenomena.

As we look back on the history of parapsychology, it is clear that this field has always existed at the margins of science, challenging conventional wisdom and pushing the boundaries of what we consider possible. Whether or not psi phenomena ultimately prove to be real, the history of their investigation offers valuable insights into the nature of scientific inquiry, the limits of empirical knowledge, and the enduring human fascination with the mysteries of the mind.

1.3 Key Phenomena in Parapsychology

Parapsychology encompasses a range of phenomena that challenge conventional scientific understanding. These fundamental phenomena are often grouped under the umbrella term "psi," which refers to the processes of information or influence that do not rely on known physical mechanisms. The main categories of psi phenomena include telepathy, psychokinesis, clairvoyance, and precognition, each of which has been the subject of extensive research and debate.

Telepathy involves directly communicating thoughts or information from one person to another without using known sensory channels. This phenomenon is the most widely recognized and studied aspect of parapsychology. Early experiments with telepathy, such as those conducted by J. B. Rhine using Zener cards, sought to provide empirical evidence for mind-to-mind communication. Modern research has continued to explore telepathy using advanced methodologies, including Ganzfeld experiments, which attempt to create conditions conducive to telepathic communication by reducing sensory input.

Psychokinesis (PK), or telekinesis, refers to the mind's ability to influence physical objects or events without physical interaction. This phenomenon has been explored in various contexts, from manipulating small objects to influencing random number generators (RNGs) in laboratory settings. While the evidence for PK remains controversial, some meta-analyses suggest small but significant effects that cannot be easily explained by chance. Researchers have proposed various models to explain PK, including the possibility that consciousness interacts with quantum processes to produce these effects.

Clairvoyance is the ability to perceive distant or hidden objects, locations, or events without using the known senses. Often referred to as "remote viewing" in modern research, clairvoyance has been studied extensively in controlled experiments. The Stargate Project, a U.S. government-funded program, conducted some of the most well-known remote viewing experiments, where individuals attempted to describe locations or events they could not physically see. While some experiments produced results that defy chance, skeptics argue that these findings could be due to methodological flaws or statistical anomalies.

Precognition involves the ability to perceive or predict future events before they occur. This phenomenon challenges the conventional understanding of time and causality, suggesting that information about the future can be accessed in the present. Precognition has been studied through experiments designed to test whether individuals can predict the outcome of random events, such as the roll of a die or the results of a card draw. While some studies have reported statistically significant results, the evidence for precognition remains highly debated, with critics pointing to issues such as the "file drawer problem" and the difficulty of replicating positive findings. The "file drawer problem," also known as publication bias, refers to the tendency of researchers to publish positive or significant results more frequently than negative or non-significant ones.

In addition to these core phenomena, parapsychology also explores experiences such as **out-of-body experiences (OBEs)**, where individuals report perceiving the world from a vantage point outside their physical bodies, and **near-death experiences (NDEs)**, where people who have been close to death report vivid, often transformative experiences that suggest consciousness may continue beyond bodily death. These experiences, while frequently reported anecdotally, have also been the subject of systematic study, with researchers attempting to determine whether they can be explained by physiological processes alone or whether they suggest the existence of a non-physical aspect of consciousness.

Each of these phenomena raises profound questions about the nature of consciousness and its relationship to the physical world. If psi phenomena are natural, they would imply that the mind is not confined to the brain and may have capabilities that extend beyond the limitations of the known physical senses. This possibility challenges the materialist paradigm that has dominated science for centuries and opens up new avenues for exploring the mysteries of human consciousness.

As researchers continue to investigate these phenomena, they face the dual challenge of producing evidence that meets the rigorous standards of scientific inquiry while also developing theoretical models that can explain how such phenomena might occur. Whether these efforts will ultimately lead to a paradigm shift in our understanding of the mind and reality remains to be seen. Still, studying psi phenomena remains a frontier of scientific exploration that invites us to reconsider what we know about the human experience.

1.4 The Scientific Method and Parapsychology

Parapsychology's exploration of phenomena that challenge the boundaries of conventional science necessitates a careful application of the scientific method. The scientific method, characterized by systematic observation, experimentation, and analysis, is the cornerstone of empirical inquiry across all disciplines. However, applying this method in parapsychology is uniquely challenging due to the elusive nature of psi phenomena.

One of the fundamental principles of the scientific method is **falsifiability**, a concept popularized by philosopher Karl Popper. For a hypothesis to be considered scientific, it must be testable and potentially disprovable. This principle poses a significant challenge for parapsychology, where many psi phenomena are difficult to replicate consistently under controlled conditions. Despite this, researchers in the field have developed rigorous protocols to test hypotheses related to psi phenomena, often going to great lengths to control for potential sources of error and bias.

Reproducibility, often confused with replication, is another critical aspect of the scientific method that has proven challenging in parapsychology. Parapsychology experiments are usually accessible to replicate, involving, for example, a subject guessing what Zener card will be drawn next when neither the experimenter nor the subject knows what it is. However, the ability to consistently replicate experimental conditions is an essential component of the scientific method. In parapsychology, however, replication has been relatively easy, with many studies yielding positive results that later prove difficult to reproduce. The challenge has been that, in many instances, after replicating the experimental conditions, the experiment fails to reproduce the initial result. This has led to ongoing debates within the scientific community about parapsychological research's reliability and the existence of psi phenomena.

To address these challenges, parapsychologists have employed increasingly sophisticated statistical techniques, such as **meta-analysis**, to assess the cumulative evidence for psi phenomena across multiple studies. Meta-analyses allow researchers to aggregate data from different experiments, increasing the statistical power and providing a more comprehensive assessment of the evidence. For example, meta-analyses of Ganzfeld experiments have been conducted to determine whether the overall effect size is significant enough to suggest the presence of telepathy.

Another critical aspect of the scientific method in parapsychology is the use of **double-blind** procedures. In a double-blind experiment, neither the participants nor the experimenters know which conditions are being tested, reducing the risk of bias. This method is particularly crucial in parapsychology, where the subjective nature of psi experiences can make the results highly susceptible to suggestion or expectation. Double-blind protocols help ensure the results are as objective as possible, minimizing the influence of the experimenter's or participant's beliefs on the outcomes.

Despite these efforts to adhere to the scientific method, parapsychology continues to face skepticism from the broader scientific community. Critics argue that the field lacks a coherent theoretical framework to explain how psi phenomena could occur within the known laws of physics. Without such a framework, they contend, the positive results reported in parapsychological research are more likely to result from methodological flaws, statistical artifacts, or even fraud rather than evidence of genuine paranormal phenomena.

However, proponents of parapsychology argue that the field's challenges only sometimes invalidate the phenomena being studied. They point out that other scientific fields have also faced difficulties developing reliable methods for analyzing complex or poorly understood phenomena. For example, the early study of electricity and magnetism encountered significant obstacles before developing robust experimental techniques and theoretical models. Parapsychologists suggest that psi phenomena may similarly require new methods and paradigms to be fully understood.

In conclusion, applying the scientific method in parapsychology is both a strength and a challenge for the field. While the rigorous testing of hypotheses and the use of advanced statistical techniques lend credibility to the research, the difficulties in replication and the lack of a clear theoretical framework continue to fuel skepticism. As the field evolves, ongoing efforts to refine methodologies and explore new theoretical models may help bridge the gap between parapsychology and mainstream science, ultimately leading to a deeper understanding of the phenomena at the heart of this controversial field.

1.5 Challenges and Controversies

Despite its long history and continued exploration of psi phenomena, parapsychology remains one of the most controversial fields within science. The challenges parapsychologists face are multifaceted, ranging from methodological difficulties to philosophical objections and the broader issue of scientific legitimacy.

Methodological Challenges: One of the most significant challenges in parapsychology is the **reproducibility** of experimental results. In mainstream science, the ability to replicate findings consistently across different studies and by independent researchers is a cornerstone of scientific validation. However, psi phenomena often exhibit variability that makes successful replication difficult, leading to questions about the reliability of positive findings. Critics argue that consistent reproducibility is necessary for the results of parapsychological research to be considered scientifically robust.

In response to these concerns, parapsychologists have developed more rigorous experimental protocols, such as those used in **meta-analyses** and **randomized controlled trials (RCTs)**. These methods aggregate data across multiple studies to identify consistent patterns that must be included in individual experiments. For example, meta-analyses of Ganzfeld experiments have suggested that, when viewed collectively, the data provides evidence for telepathy despite the challenges of replicability in individual studies.

Statistical Issues: Another controversy in parapsychology revolves around the interpretation of statistical data. Since psi effects are often subtle, researchers must rely on statistical analyses to determine whether observed effects are genuinely anomalous or simply due to chance. However, statistical anomalies can occur for various reasons, including methodological flaws, bias, or even the misuse of statistical techniques. Critics have argued that relying on statistical significance in parapsychology can sometimes lead to overinterpreting weak effects, giving the appearance of evidence where none may exist.

Philosophical and Theoretical Challenges: Beyond the methodological and statistical issues, parapsychology faces significant philosophical challenges. One of the most prominent is the need for **a comprehensive theoretical framework** explaining how psi phenomena could occur within the known laws of physics. While some researchers have proposed connections between psi and quantum mechanics, these ideas remain speculative and are not widely accepted within the broader scientific community.

A widely accepted theory is necessary to place psi phenomena within the context of established scientific knowledge. Without a clear theoretical foundation, the positive results of parapsychological research are often viewed with skepticism, as they seem to contradict the current understanding of the physical world. This has led to ongoing debates about whether parapsychology should be considered a legitimate scientific discipline or whether it falls outside the boundaries of science as traditionally defined.

Skepticism and the Scientific Community: The skepticism surrounding parapsychology is not limited to methodological or theoretical concerns. Associations with pseudoscience and sensationalism have also marred the field and, in some cases, outright fraud. High-profile cases of fraud in parapsychology, such as the exposure of fraudulent mediums in the early 20th century, have contributed to a general mistrust of the field. This has made it difficult for parapsychologists to gain acceptance within the broader scientific community, as the field is often dismissed as unscientific or even as a form of entertainment rather than serious inquiry.

In addition, the **media portrayal** of parapsychology often sensationalizes psi phenomena, focusing on the more extraordinary claims rather than the careful, controlled research conducted by serious scientists. This has further fueled skepticism and led to a public perception of parapsychology often more aligned with fiction than science.

The Role of Experimenter Bias: Experimenter bias is another significant challenge in parapsychology. This refers to the potential for researchers' expectations, beliefs, or desires to influence the outcomes of their experiments unconsciously. Given the subjective nature of many psi phenomena, such as telepathy or clairvoyance, there is a heightened risk of bias affecting the results. To mitigate this, parapsychologists have increasingly adopted **double-blind protocols**, where neither the participants nor the experimenters know the specific conditions being tested. However, even with these precautions, the possibility of subtle biases influencing the results remains a concern.

Ethical Considerations: Finally, exploring psi phenomena raises critical ethical questions, particularly regarding the potential applications of these abilities. For instance, if psi phenomena such as telepathy or remote viewing were proven genuine and could be harnessed reliably, they could have significant implications for privacy, security, and personal autonomy. These ethical considerations add another layer of complexity to the field, as researchers must balance the pursuit of knowledge with the potential risks associated with their findings.

In conclusion, parapsychology is a field that exists at the intersection of science, philosophy, and the unknown. While it faces significant challenges and controversies, these obstacles make studying psi phenomena intriguing and potentially transformative. As researchers refine their methods and explore new theoretical possibilities, the ongoing debate about parapsychology will likely remain a dynamic and evolving conversation within the broader scientific community.

1.6 The Importance of Parapsychology

Parapsychology is uniquely positioned in scientific inquiry, offering profound challenges and opportunities. Its importance lies in the potential to uncover new aspects of human consciousness and its ability to push the boundaries of what we consider possible within the natural world. The study of psi phenomena invites us to explore the limits of our scientific and philosophical understanding, raising questions about the nature of reality, consciousness, and the mind's potential.

One of parapsychology's critical contributions is expanding the scope of scientific investigation. While mainstream science tends to focus on phenomena that can be explained within the existing framework of physical laws, parapsychology challenges these boundaries by investigating experiences that defy conventional explanations. This willingness to explore the unknown has led to the development of new experimental methods and theoretical models, some of which have potential applications beyond parapsychology.

For instance, using rigorous statistical techniques, such as meta-analysis, in parapsychology has influenced other fields of study, particularly in areas where effects are subtle and complex to measure. Exploring psi phenomena has also prompted researchers to reconsider the nature of consciousness and its relationship to the physical world. This has led to interdisciplinary collaborations with fields such as quantum physics, neuroscience, and psychology, fostering a more holistic approach to understanding human experience.

Moreover, parapsychology encourages a re-examination of the philosophical foundations of science. By investigating phenomena that challenge materialism and reductionism, parapsychology invites a broader discussion about the limits of scientific knowledge and the potential for alternative paradigms. This has significant implications for our understanding of consciousness and wider questions about the nature of reality and the universe.

Another critical aspect of parapsychology is its potential impact on our understanding of human potential. If psi phenomena are proven genuine, they would suggest that the mind is capable of much more than what is currently understood. This could lead to new approaches in fields such as psychology, education, and even medicine, where the power of the mind might be harnessed in ways that are currently unimaginable.

Furthermore, parapsychology has cultural and societal significance. Throughout history, humans have reported experiences that transcend the physical world, from telepathic communication to premonitions of future events. These experiences, often dismissed or marginalized, have persisted across cultures and epochs. By studying these phenomena scientifically, parapsychology provides a framework for understanding these experiences, potentially validating the experiences of countless individuals who have reported psi events.

In a broader sense, parapsychology challenges the dichotomy between science and spirituality. The study of psi phenomena bridges these two domains in many ways, suggesting that aspects of reality may be accessible through empirical investigation and spiritual insight. This convergence could lead to a more integrated understanding of the world, where science and spirituality are seen not as opposing forces but as complementary ways of knowing.

In conclusion, parapsychology's importance extends far beyond studying psi phenomena. It lies in the field's ability to push the boundaries of scientific inquiry, challenge our assumptions about the nature of consciousness and reality, and open up new possibilities for understanding the human experience. As research in parapsychology continues to evolve, its contributions to science, philosophy, and society will likely become increasingly significant, offering new insights into the mysteries of the mind and the universe.

2

TELEPATHY: MIND-TO-MIND COMMUNICATION

2.1 Introduction to Telepathy

Telepathy, often called "mind-to-mind" communication, is one of parapsychology's most compelling and widely recognized phenomena. It involves the direct transfer of thoughts, feelings, or information between individuals without known sensory channels or physical interaction. Telepathy has been reported in various cultural contexts throughout history, often attributed to mystical or supernatural abilities. However, in the modern era, telepathy has become the subject of systematic scientific investigation, with researchers seeking to determine whether such a phenomenon can be reliably demonstrated and understood within a scientific framework.

The allure of telepathy lies in its potential to fundamentally alter our understanding of communication and consciousness. If telepathy were proven to exist, the mind would have capabilities far beyond what is currently recognized by mainstream science. It would challenge the conventional view of the brain as the sole generator of thoughts and open new avenues for exploring the nature of consciousness and its connection to the broader universe.

In this chapter, we will review the scientific study of telepathy, exploring its historical background, key experiments, theoretical models, and the ongoing debates surrounding its validity. We will also examine telepathy's potential implications for our understanding of the human mind and the possibilities it raises for future research in parapsychology and related fields.

2.2 Historical Accounts of Telepathy

Telepathy has deep roots in human history, with accounts of mind-to-mind communication appearing in ancient texts, religious scriptures, and folklore. In many ancient cultures, telepathic abilities were attributed to gods, shamans, or spiritual leaders believed to possess special powers that allowed them to communicate across distances without physical interaction.

In ancient Greece, for example, the Oracle of Delphi was said to receive messages from the gods, often interpreted as telepathic communications. Similarly, in Hindu scriptures, "manas" (mind) includes the ability to perceive thoughts and emotions directly, aligning with modern telepathy understandings. Indigenous cultures worldwide have also reported telepathic communication, often as part of spiritual or healing practices.

The modern study of telepathy began in the late 19th century, during a period of intense interest in the paranormal and spiritualism. The Society for Psychical Research (SPR) in London played a pivotal role in bringing telepathy into the realm of scientific inquiry. Early researchers, such as Frederic W. H. Myers and William Barrett, conducted experiments to test the validity of telepathic claims, using methods that laid the groundwork for future studies.

One of the most famous early cases of telepathy investigated by the SPR was the "Cross-Correspondences," a series of communications purportedly received by multiple mediums that were said to originate from deceased members of the SPR. These communications were believed to be an attempt by the deceased to prove the reality of telepathy and life after death. While the case remains controversial, it sparked significant interest and debate.

The early 20th century saw the rise of more controlled experiments in telepathy, with researchers like J. B. Rhine at Duke University conducting systematic studies using Zener cards. These experiments aimed to provide empirical evidence for telepathy by testing whether participants could accurately perceive symbols or images "sent" by another person without any sensory cues. Rhine's work brought telepathy into the mainstream of parapsychological research, although it also faced criticism for methodological flaws and issues with reproducibility.

As we explore these historical accounts, it becomes clear that telepathy has been a topic of fascination for centuries, inspiring both belief and skepticism. The transition from anecdotal reports to controlled scientific studies marks a significant evolution in the investigation of telepathy, one that continues to shape our understanding of this enigmatic phenomenon.

2.3 Scientific Investigations into Telepathy

The scientific investigation of telepathy has evolved significantly since its early days, with researchers employing increasingly sophisticated methods to test the phenomenon under controlled conditions. These studies aim to determine whether telepathy can be demonstrated reliably and, if so, to understand its underlying mechanisms.

The Ganzfeld experiment is one of the most well-known and widely used experimental paradigms for studying telepathy. Developed in the 1970s by Charles Honorton and others, the Ganzfeld technique involves placing a "receiver" in a state of sensory deprivation. At the same time, a "sender" attempts to transmit specific information, such as an image or video, to the receiver. The receiver, isolated from external stimuli, describes any impressions or images that come to mind, which are then compared to the target material. Over the years, meta-analyses of Ganzfeld experiments have shown statistically significant results, suggesting that telepathic communication may occur. However, skeptics argue that these findings could be due to methodological flaws or biases (Honorton & Ferrari, 1989).

Another critical area of research in telepathy involves using **random number generators (RNGs)** to test whether participants can influence or predict sequences of random numbers generated by a machine. While not directly related to telepathy in the traditional sense, these studies explore the broader category of mind-matter interaction, which includes telepathic communication as a potential manifestation of such interactions. The results of RNG studies have been mixed, with some researchers reporting significant effects while others still need to reproduce these findings (Schmidt, 1976; Bösch et al., 2006).

Neuroscientific approaches to telepathy have also emerged, with researchers using brain imaging techniques, such as functional magnetic resonance imaging (fMRI) and electroencephalography (EEG), to study the brain activity of individuals during telepathic tasks. These studies aim to identify specific neural correlates of telepathic communication and determine whether brain activity patterns are associated with successful telepathic transmission. Although these studies are still in their early stages, they represent a promising direction for future research, as they may help bridge the gap between subjective experiences of telepathy and objective scientific evidence (Persinger, 2008; Tart, 2009).

Another notable area of investigation is **quantum entanglement**, a phenomenon in quantum physics where particles become interconnected so that one particle's state instantly influences another's state, regardless of distance. Some theorists have speculated that telepathy could be related to quantum entanglement, suggesting that the minds of individuals might become "entangled" similarly, allowing for instantaneous communication across distances. While this idea remains speculative, it has sparked interest among physicists and parapsychologists as a potential explanation for telepathy (Goswami, 1993; Radin, 2006).

Despite the advances in experimental methods and technology, the scientific study of telepathy continues to face significant challenges. **Replication** or reproducibility remains a major issue, with many studies failing to produce consistent results when conducted by independent researchers. Additionally, the need for a widely accepted theoretical framework for telepathy makes it challenging to interpret positive findings and integrate them into the broader body of scientific knowledge.

Nevertheless, the ongoing investigation of telepathy is essential for several reasons. First, it pushes the boundaries of what we consider possible within the realm of human experience, challenging the materialist assumptions that dominate much of contemporary science. Second, it opens up new avenues for exploring the nature of consciousness and the potential for non-local connections between minds. Finally, the study of telepathy has broader implications for our understanding of communication, suggesting that the mind may possess untapped abilities that could revolutionize how we interact.

As research in this field continues, new methodologies, technologies, and theoretical models will likely emerge, offering fresh insights into the phenomenon of telepathy and its potential role in the broader landscape of human consciousness.

2.4 Experimental Methods in Telepathy Research

The study of telepathy has seen the development of various experimental methods designed to test the phenomenon under controlled conditions. These methods aim to eliminate alternative explanations, such as sensory leakage, chance, or experimenter bias, and to provide reliable evidence of telepathic communication.

One of the most prominent methods is the **Ganzfeld experiment**, which has become a standard in telepathy research. In a typical Ganzfeld experiment, a "receiver" is placed in a state of sensory deprivation, often achieved by covering their eyes with halves of ping-pong balls, using red light to create a uniform visual field, and playing white noise through headphones. This setup is intended to minimize sensory input and enhance the receiver's ability to detect telepathic signals. Meanwhile, a "sender" is located in a separate room and attempts to transmit a target image or video to the receiver mentally. After the session, the receiver is shown several images or videos, including the target, and asked to identify which one they believe was sent. The rate of correct identifications is then compared to what would be expected by chance (Bem & Honorton, 1994).

Remote viewing is another experimental method used in telepathy research, though it is more often associated with divination. In remote viewing experiments, a subject attempts to describe or sketch details of a distant location or object they have never seen before. The target is typically selected randomly and unknown to the subject and the experimenter. The accuracy of the subject's description is then assessed by comparing it to the target (May 1996).

A lesser-known but intriguing method is the **use of twins** in telepathy research. Some studies have focused on identical twins, who often report having a deep psychological connection. Researchers have conducted experiments where one twin, isolated in a separate room, is subjected to a stimulus (e.g., a light flash or an emotional image). In contrast, the other twin, who is not exposed to the stimulus, is monitored for physiological responses such as changes in heart rate or skin conductance. The goal is to determine whether the non-exposed twin exhibits any physiological changes that could suggest telepathic communication. While results have been mixed, some studies have reported significant correlations between the twins' responses (Radin, 2006).

Statistical methods also play a crucial role in telepathy research. Given the subtle nature of psi effects, researchers often rely on statistical analyses to determine whether their findings are anomalous or simply due to chance. This includes using **meta-analysis**, which aggregates data from multiple studies to assess the overall evidence for telepathy. Meta-analyses can provide a more comprehensive picture by increasing statistical power and highlighting patterns that might not be evident in individual studies.

Another experimental approach uses **random number generators (RNGs)** in telepathy experiments. In these studies, a receiver attempts to predict or influence the outcome of a random number sequence generated by a machine. The results are then compared to what would be expected by chance. Although RNG studies are more commonly associated with psychokinesis research, they have also been used to explore the potential for telepathic influence over random processes (Bösch et al., 2006).

Despite these methodological advancements, telepathy research remains controversial. Critics argue that the effects observed in these experiments are often small and difficult to replicate and that alternative explanations, such as sensory leakage or experimenter bias, can only sometimes be ruled out. Additionally, the **file drawer problem**, where studies with null results are less likely to be published, may contribute to overestimating the evidence for telepathy.

Nevertheless, developing these experimental methods represents significant progress in the scientific investigation of telepathy. By continuing to refine these techniques and address the challenges inherent in psi research, scientists can provide more definitive answers about the reality and mechanisms of telepathic communication.

2.5 Famous Telepathy Experiments

The history of telepathy research is marked by several landmark experiments that have shaped the field, each contributing to our understanding of this enigmatic phenomenon. These experiments, conducted over the past century, have sparked both interest and controversy, serving as key reference points in the ongoing debate over the existence and nature of telepathic communication.

One of the earliest and most influential experiments was the **"Smith-Blackburn telepathy test"** conducted by the Society for Psychical Research (SPR) in the late 19th century. This experiment systematically studied telepathic communication between a "sender" and a "receiver" in separate rooms. The experimenters sought to eliminate all possible sensory cues, ensuring that any communication could only occur through telepathy. While the results were inconclusive, they provided early evidence that telepathy might be a natural phenomenon, laying the groundwork for future research.

In the 1930s, **J. B. Rhine's experiments at Duke University** became another milestone in telepathy research. Using Zener cards —a deck of 25 cards featuring five different symbols—Rhine tested whether participants could correctly identify the symbol on a card held by a sender in another room. Rhine's results, which suggested that some individuals could identify the symbols at rates higher than chance, were groundbreaking at the time and helped establish parapsychology as a legitimate field of study. However, Rhine's work also attracted criticism, with skeptics questioning the statistical methods used and the potential for sensory leakage (Rhine, 1937).

A more recent and widely cited series of experiments is the **Ganzfeld studies**, which were initiated in the 1970s by parapsychologist Charles Honorton. The Ganzfeld experiments are considered one of the most rigorous and well-controlled telepathy studies. As previously mentioned, these experiments involve placing a receiver in a state of sensory deprivation while a sender attempts to transmit a target image or video. Honorton's meta-analysis of these studies, published in the 1980s, reported a statistically significant effect, suggesting that telepathy might occur under certain conditions. Other researchers have replicated the results of the Ganzfeld experiments, although the degree of replication has been a matter of ongoing debate (Bem & Honorton, 1994).

The **Stargate Project**, a secret U.S. government program from the 1970s to the 1990s, also significantly contributed to telepathy research, albeit in a classified context. The project aimed to investigate the potential use of remote viewing and telepathy for military and intelligence purposes. While much of the research focused on remote viewing, some aspects of the program involved testing for telepathic abilities. The results of the Stargate Project were mixed, leading to the eventual closure of the program. Still, the experiments conducted during this period continue to be cited in discussions of telepathy and related phenomena (May 1996).

Another critical study is the **"Maimonides Dream Telepathy" experiments** conducted at the Maimonides Medical Center in Brooklyn in the 1960s and 1970s. In these experiments, a sender attempted to transmit a target image to a receiver in the Rapid Eye Movement (REM) stage of sleep. The receiver's dreams were then analyzed to see if they contained elements of the target image. The results of these studies were promising, showing higher-than-chance correspondences between the targets and the dream content, suggesting that telepathy might occur during sleep (Utts, 1995; Radin, 1997).

Utts (1995) reviews the evidence for psychic phenomena, including dream telepathy, focusing on experiments conducted at the Maimonides Medical Center in the 1960s and 1970s. These experiments aimed to test whether a "sender" could influence the dreams of a "receiver" under controlled conditions. The results provided some evidence supporting telepathy, though they have been subject to debate and calls for further replication.

These famous experiments have played a crucial role in shaping telepathy research. They have provided evidence that, while not universally accepted, continues to fuel the debate over the existence and mechanisms of telepathy. Each of these experiments has contributed to refining research methodologies, highlighting the importance of rigorous controls, and encouraging the development of new theories to explain how telepathic communication might occur.

2.6 Theoretical Explanations for Telepathy

The theoretical underpinnings of telepathy have long been a subject of speculation and debate within parapsychology and related fields. While telepathy has yet to be fully explained within the framework of conventional science, several theories have been proposed to account for the phenomenon. These theories range from psychological models to those that invoke quantum mechanics and other aspects of modern physics.

Psychological Theories: Some of the earliest explanations for telepathy were grounded in psychology. For instance, the concept of the **unconscious mind, as proposed by Sigmund Freud and Carl Jung,** has been used to suggest that telepathy could occur due to deep, unconscious connections between individuals. Jung's idea of the **collective unconscious,** a shared repository of human experiences and memories, could provide a medium for telepathic communication. In this view, telepathy might manifest the mind's ability to tap into this collective pool of knowledge and emotions.

Electromagnetic Theories: Another line of thought is that electromagnetic fields or waves could mediate telepathy. Early researchers speculated that the brain might emit and receive electromagnetic signals that could account for telepathic communication. However, as our understanding of electromagnetic fields has advanced, this theory has faced significant challenges, particularly the need for empirical evidence supporting the idea that the brain generates or responds to electromagnetic waves in a way that would facilitate telepathy.

Persinger (2008) explores the possibility that telepathy and other psi phenomena could be mediated by electromagnetic fields, specifically through the synchronization of brain waves between individuals. He proposes that certain brain activities might synchronize under specific conditions, allowing for the direct transmission of thoughts or feelings and providing a potential neuroscientific basis for telepathy.

Quantum Theories: One more recent and intriguing approach to explaining telepathy involves **quantum mechanics.** The concept of **quantum entanglement,** where two or more particles become linked and instantaneously affect each other regardless of distance, has been proposed as a potential mechanism for telepathy. Some researchers hypothesize that human consciousness might be capable of interacting with the quantum field, allowing information to be shared non-locally between individuals. This theory remains speculative, as it extends quantum principles from the subatomic level to the macroscopic level of human consciousness, a leap that still needs to be supported by empirical evidence (Radin, 2006).

Field Theories: Another perspective is the idea of a "**psi field**" or a **morphic field**, as proposed by biologist Rupert Sheldrake (1981, 2009). Sheldrake's theory of **morphic resonance** suggests that all living organisms are connected by fields of information that transcend space and time. According to this theory, telepathy could occur through resonance within these fields, where similar patterns of thought or behavior in one individual can influence another across distances. While intriguing, this theory is controversial and has yet to gain widespread acceptance in the scientific community.

One of the most cited examples of morphic resonance involves laboratory rats learning a new behavior, such as navigating a maze. According to Sheldrake, once rats in one location learn to navigate the maze, subsequent generations of rats—even those in different locations—should learn the maze more quickly due to the resonance of the morphic field associated with that learned behavior. In other words, the knowledge the first group of rats gains creates a morphic field that other rats can tap into, leading to quicker learning. This example often illustrates how information might be stored non-locally and accessed across time and space, challenging conventional views of biology and learning.

Neurological Theories: Some researchers have also explored the possibility of telepathy being linked to specific brain functions or states of consciousness. **Neuroscientific studies** using tools like EEG and fMRI have sought to identify neural correlates of telepathic communication, looking for patterns of brain activity that might indicate a telepathic connection. While these studies have yet to produce definitive evidence, they suggest that certain brain states, possibly related to altered states of consciousness or meditation, might facilitate telepathic experiences.

Sociocultural Theories: Besides these scientific theories, some have suggested that telepathy might be a culturally constructed phenomenon, where social and cultural factors influence the percep-

tion and reporting of telepathic experiences. This perspective emphasizes the role of expectation, belief, and suggestion in shaping
telepathic reports, suggesting that what is perceived as telepathy
might sometimes result from psychological or cultural factors rather
than an actual transmission of information.

Each of these theories offers a different lens through which to
view telepathy, reflecting the phenomenon's complexity and
interdisciplinary nature. While no single theory has emerged as a
definitive explanation, the ongoing exploration of these ideas
continues to push the boundaries of our understanding of consciousness, communication, and the nature of reality itself.

2.7 Challenges and Criticisms

Like other parapsychology areas, telepathy studies face significant
challenges and criticisms that have shaped the field's development
and reception within the broader scientific community. These
multifaceted challenges involve methodological issues, replicability
concerns, and philosophical objections, creating a complex landscape for researchers to navigate.

Methodological Challenges: One of the primary criticisms of
telepathy research is the **methodological rigor** of experiments.
Critics argue that many early studies, and even some contemporary
ones, suffer from flaws such as inadequate controls, potential sensory
leakage, and the influence of experimenter bias. For example, in
some telepathy experiments, ensuring that the receiver is not unconsciously picking up on subtle cues from the sender or the environment has been challenging, which could account for seemingly
telepathic results. To address these concerns, researchers have
increasingly employed more sophisticated techniques, such as
double-blind protocols and automated randomization, to minimize
potential sources of bias and error.

Replicability Issues: Another significant challenge in telepathy
research is **replication**. In science, the ability to replicate findings
across different studies and by independent researchers is a corner-

stone of establishing the validity of a phenomenon. However, telepathy experiments have often struggled with replicability, with many studies failing to produce consistent results. This has led to skepticism within the scientific community, with critics arguing that positive findings in telepathy research may result from chance, selective reporting, or subtle methodological flaws rather than evidence of a genuine phenomenon.

The **file drawer problem**—the tendency for studies with null results to remain unpublished—exacerbates the replicability issue. This phenomenon can create a biased impression of the evidence for telepathy, as studies that do not support the existence of telepathy are less likely to be reported. At the same time, positive results are more likely to be published and cited. Meta-analyses attempt to address this issue by including published and unpublished studies, but the file drawer problem remains a persistent challenge in the field.

Statistical Criticisms: The reliance on **statistical significance** in telepathy research has also been a point of contention. Given the subtle and often weak effects reported in telepathy studies, researchers must use statistical methods to determine whether their findings significantly differ from what would be expected by chance. However, critics argue that the small effect sizes commonly reported in telepathy studies are susceptible to issues such as **p-hacking** (the manipulation of data to achieve statistical significance) and **overfitting** (creating models that fit the data too closely without accounting for underlying patterns). These concerns have led some to question whether the statistical evidence for telepathy is robust enough to support the claims made by researchers.

Philosophical Objections: Beyond methodological and statistical issues, telepathy research faces philosophical objections that challenge the plausibility of the phenomenon itself. Many critics argue that telepathy, as traditionally conceived, is incompatible with our current understanding of the brain and the physical laws that govern information transfer. Without a coherent theoretical framework that explains how thoughts or information could be transmitted without any physical medium, skeptics remain doubtful about the reality of telepathy.

Moreover, the **materialist paradigm** that dominates much of modern science posits that all mental processes are ultimately the result of physical interactions within the brain. From this perspective, the idea that thoughts or emotions could be transmitted telepathically, without any physical intermediary, seems implausible. This philosophical stance has contributed to the marginalization of telepathy research within mainstream science, as many researchers are reluctant to engage with a phenomenon that appears to conflict with established scientific principles.

Cultural and Social Criticisms: Telepathy research is subject to **cultural and social criticisms.** In popular culture, telepathy is often associated with pseudoscience, fantasy, and the paranormal, leading to a perception that the field lacks scientific credibility. This perception is reinforced by the association of telepathy with sensational claims and unverified anecdotes, which detract from the more rigorous scientific studies conducted by serious researchers.

The portrayal of telepathy in the media, where it is often sensationalized or trivialized, further complicates the field's reputation. This has created a challenging environment for researchers, who must address the scientific challenges of studying telepathy and contend with the broader public's skepticism and misunderstanding of the field.

Ethical Considerations: The potential implications of proving telepathy also raise **ethical concerns.** If telepathy were demonstrated to be a natural and reliable ability, it would raise significant questions about privacy and consent. The idea that one's thoughts or emotions could be accessed without their knowledge or permission could lead to profound ethical dilemmas, particularly in national security, personal relationships, and mental health.

In conclusion, the challenges and criticisms of telepathy research are substantial, reflecting the complexities of investigating a phenomenon at the intersection of science, philosophy, and culture. While these challenges have hindered the acceptance of telepathy within mainstream science, they have also driven researchers to develop more rigorous methodologies and to engage in deeper theoretical and philosophical exploration. As the field evolves, addressing these challenges will be crucial for advancing our understanding of telepathy and its potential role in the broader landscape of human consciousness.

2.8 Applications of Telepathy

If telepathy were proven to be a reliable and replicable phenomenon, it could have profound implications for various fields, ranging from communication to medicine. While much of the current research remains speculative, several potential applications of telepathy are worth exploring.

Communication: Telepathy would be the most apparent application as a novel form of communication. Telepathy could allow for direct mind-to-mind communication, bypassing the need for spoken or written language. This could be particularly beneficial for individuals with communication disabilities, such as those who are nonverbal or have conditions that impair speech. Additionally, telepathy could facilitate communication in situations where traditional methods are impractical, such as in environments with significant noise or remote locations where technology-based communication might fail.

Therapeutic Applications: Telepathy could revolutionize therapy and counseling in mental health. If therapists could directly perceive the thoughts and emotions of their patients, it could lead to more accurate diagnoses and more personalized treatment plans. Telepathy might also enhance empathy and understanding in therapeutic relationships, helping therapists connect with patients more deeply. Moreover, telepathy could provide a way to reach individuals unable or unwilling to articulate their thoughts and feelings verbally, offering a new avenue for psychological support.

Education: Telepathy could transform education by enabling the direct transmission of knowledge and skills from teacher to student.

This could lead to more efficient learning processes, where complex concepts are communicated directly without the potential for misunderstanding or misinterpretation. Additionally, telepathy could support collaborative learning, allowing students to share ideas and insights instantaneously and fostering a more dynamic and interactive educational environment.

Creative Collaboration: In the arts and creative industries, telepathy could facilitate deeper and more intuitive collaboration between artists, writers, musicians, and other creative professionals. By directly sharing thoughts, ideas, and visions, collaborators could achieve a level of synergy that transcends traditional communication methods, potentially leading to more innovative and cohesive creative outputs.

Security and Intelligence: In security and intelligence, telepathy could be used to gather information when traditional methods are limited. For example, telepathic abilities could be employed in counterterrorism efforts, where the ability to perceive the intentions of individuals or groups could prevent potential threats. However, this application raises significant ethical concerns regarding privacy and possible misuse.

Military Applications: The potential military applications of telepathy have been a subject of interest, as evidenced by the U.S. government's Stargate Project, which investigated the use of psychic abilities for espionage and intelligence gathering. If telepathy could be harnessed reliably, it might be used for communication between soldiers in the field without needing electronic devices, which could be intercepted or jammed by the enemy. Telepathic communication could also play a role in strategic planning, allowing for instant and secure exchange of information between military leaders.

Human-Machine Interaction: Another intriguing possibility is the application of telepathy in human-machine interaction. If telepathic communication with machines or artificial intelligence systems were possible, it could lead to a new era of human-computer interfaces where thoughts alone control devices, enhancing efficiency and accessibility. This could have significant implications for individuals with disabilities, allowing them to interact with technology in currently impossible ways.

Ethical and Social Implications: Telepathy's potential applications are vast and varied, but they also raise significant moral and social questions. Privacy, consent, and the potential for exploitation must be carefully considered as the field advances. The ability to access another person's thoughts or emotions without their permission could lead to significant breaches of privacy and autonomy, necessitating the development of strict ethical guidelines and safeguards.

In conclusion, while the practical applications of telepathy remain speculative at this stage, the possibilities are both exciting and daunting. As research continues, it is essential to consider the potential benefits and the ethical implications of harnessing telepathy for various purposes. Whether telepathy can be proven and developed into a practical tool remains to be seen. Still, exploring its potential applications continues to be a fascinating and vital aspect of parapsychological research.

2.9 Challenges in Reproducing ESP Research

A critical challenge in ESP research is the reproducibility of results. While some studies have reported positive findings, these results have often been difficult to replicate in subsequent experiments. This issue of reproducibility has fueled skepticism within the scientific community, as consistent replication is a cornerstone of scientific validation (Wiseman & Schlitz, 1997).

Several factors may contribute to the difficulty in replicating ESP experiments. The highly variable nature of ESP phenomena, potential experimenter effects, and subtle environmental influences could all impact the outcomes of these studies. Moreover, the subjective nature of some ESP experiences, such as telepathy or remote viewing, complicates the development of standardized experimental protocols (Schlitz & Braud, 1997).

Some researchers have advocated for more rigorous experimental designs, including double-blind protocols and more sophisticated statistical analyses to address these challenges. These measures aim to reduce the potential for bias.

2.10 The Role of Experimenter and Participant Variables in ESP Research

A significant aspect of ESP research is the role of experimenter and participant variables in the outcomes of studies. Experimenter effects, where the researcher's beliefs, expectations, or behaviors can inadvertently influence the results, are particularly challenging in ESP experiments. Studies have shown that experimenters who believe in the possibility of ESP are more likely to report positive results, suggesting that their expectations might subtly influence the participants or the interpretation of data (Rosenthal, 1976).

Similarly, participants' psychological and physiological characteristics can significantly impact ESP experiment outcomes. Factors such as personality traits, emotional states, and even the participant's physiological state (e.g., stress levels, brainwave patterns) have been explored as potential contributors to the variability in ESP performance. For instance, some research suggests that individuals who score high on certain personality traits, like openness to experience, might be more susceptible to experiencing ESP phenomena (Thalbourne, 1994).

Additionally, physiological factors, such as electroencephalogram (EEG) readings, have been studied to understand their relationship with ESP performance. Some researchers have hypothesized that specific brainwave patterns, such as increased alpha or theta activity, might be conducive to ESP experiences (White, 1990). However, the results of these studies could be more consistent, highlighting the complexity of identifying reliable predictors of ESP abilities.

2.11 Psi-Mediated Instrumental Response (PMIR) and Its Implications for ESP

One of the more intriguing theoretical developments in ESP research is the concept of Psi-Mediated Instrumental Response (PMIR), proposed by psychologist Rex Stanford. PMIR suggests that psi, the hypothesized underlying mechanism of ESP, functions subconsciously to help individuals achieve their goals by influencing events or acquiring information that bypasses ordinary sensory channels (Stanford, 1974).

According to PMIR theory, individuals might unknowingly use psi to gather information that helps them make decisions or avoid danger without being consciously aware of the process. This concept challenges the traditional view of ESP as a conscious, deliberate process, instead proposing that psi operates as an unconscious adaptive function. If correct, this theory could explain why ESP experiences often occur spontaneously when the individual has a strong emotional investment or need for information.

The implications of PMIR for ESP research are significant. It suggests that there are more effective ways to study the phenomenon than traditional experimental setups, which often require conscious attempts at ESP. Instead, researchers may design experiments that tap into unconscious processes by creating scenarios where participants are motivated to use psi without being explicitly aware of it.

2.12 Advances in Statistical Methods: Addressing the Issue of Multiple Comparisons

A critical concern in ESP research, as in many fields of experimental science, is the issue of multiple comparisons. When researchers conduct numerous statistical tests on the same dataset, the likelihood of finding at least one significant result purely by chance increases. This problem is particularly relevant in ESP research, where studies often involve multiple targets, sessions, or conditions, each subject to statistical analysis.

Researchers have developed more sophisticated statistical methods to address this issue and control for the increased risk of false positives due to multiple comparisons. Techniques such as the Bonferroni correction, which adjusts the significance level based on the number of comparisons, are now commonly used in ESP studies (Hyman, 1985). Additionally, Bayesian approaches have been proposed to incorporate prior knowledge and expectations into the analysis, potentially providing a more nuanced interpretation of ESP data (Utts, 1991).

In a seminal paper, Utts (1991) reviews the statistical methods used in parapsychology, focusing on the importance of replication and meta-analysis in establishing the reliability of psi phenomena. Utts critically examines the evidence from various parapsychological studies, arguing that the results are statistically significant and not easily dismissed as artifacts of chance or methodological flaws. She emphasizes the role of rigorous statistical analysis in validating para-psychological research and advocates for a more open-minded approach to studying these phenomena. This paper is a cornerstone in parapsychology, contributing to the ongoing debate about the scientific legitimacy of psi research.

These advances in statistical methodology represent an essential step forward for ESP research, helping to ensure that reported find-ings are robust and less likely to result from chance. However, the challenge of multiple comparisons remains a critical consideration in the design and interpretation of ESP experiments.

2.13 The Cultural and Psychological Context of ESP Experiences

ESP experiences do not occur in a vacuum; they are deeply embedded in cultural and psychological contexts that shape how individuals perceive and interpret these phenomena. Cultural beliefs about the paranormal and individual psychological factors play a significant role in determining who reports ESP experiences and how those experiences are understood.

For instance, in cultures where belief in the paranormal is widespread, individuals may be more likely to interpret ambiguous experiences—such as intuitive feelings, dreams, or coincidences—as evidence of ESP. Conversely, in cultures with a more skeptical or materialist worldview, the same experiences might be dismissed as mere chance or psychological aberrations (Haraldsson, 2011).

Psychological factors also influence the likelihood of reporting ESP experiences. Research has shown that individuals with high levels of anxiety, stress, or emotional sensitivity are more likely to report ESP experiences, possibly because these states heighten awareness of internal and external stimuli (Schouten, 1994). Additionally, personality traits such as openness to experience and a tendency toward fantasy-proneness have been associated with a higher incidence of reported ESP experiences (Thalbourne, 1994).

Understanding the cultural and psychological context of ESP is crucial for interpreting the findings of ESP research. It highlights the need for a multidisciplinary approach that considers the potential existence of psi phenomena and the complex interplay of belief, perception, and psychological factors that shape how these experiences are reported and understood.

2.14 The Role of Consciousness in ESP: Emerging Theories and Research

As research into ESP continues, the role of consciousness has emerged as a central theme. Theories of consciousness that extend beyond the brain's physical processes offer potential explanations for how ESP might occur. Some researchers have proposed that consciousness is a fundamental aspect of reality rather than merely a byproduct of brain activity. This perspective allows consciousness to interact with the physical world in ways not yet fully understood by mainstream science (Tart, 2009).

For example, the idea of a "universal consciousness" or "collective unconscious," as initially proposed by Carl Jung, suggests that individuals might tap into a shared reservoir of knowledge or information, which could explain phenomena such as telepathy or clairvoyance (Jung, 1973). Similarly, the notion of consciousness as a non-local phenomenon, not confined to the brain, aligns with findings from quantum physics that suggest the interconnectedness of all things at a fundamental level (Radin, 2006).

Emerging research in this area is increasingly interdisciplinary, drawing on insights from quantum physics, neurobiology, and consciousness studies. These efforts are part of a broader attempt to develop a theoretical framework that can account for the observed phenomena of ESP while also addressing the limitations and challenges of current scientific paradigms.

2.15 Psi as an Anomalous Cognition: A Paradigm Shift in Understanding ESP

The concept of "psi" has evolved as a broader term encompassing ESP, telepathy, and related phenomena. Psi is often described as an anomalous form of cognition, operating outside the bounds of normal sensory and cognitive processes. This framing represents a paradigm shift in how researchers approach the study of ESP, moving away from the idea of psi as a "supernatural" phenomenon and toward a more nuanced understanding of it as an extension of normal cognitive processes under certain conditions (Targ & Katra, 2001).

This shift in perspective has significant implications for how ESP research is conducted and interpreted. Researchers can explore psi using cognitive science, psychology, and neuroscience tools and methodologies by framing psi as a form of anomalous cognition. This approach also allows for integrating ESP research into the broader field of consciousness studies, where it can be examined alongside other non-ordinary experiences, such as altered states of consciousness, meditation, and mystical experiences.

The paradigm shift toward midderstanding psi as an aspect of cognition rather than a "paranormal" phenomenon may help bridge the gap between mainstream science and parapsychology. It opens the door to new research and theoretical development avenues while providing a framework for integrating psi phenomena into a more comprehensive understanding of human consciousness.

2.16 The Future of ESP Research: Challenges and Opportunities

The future of ESP research is full of challenges and significant opportunities for advancing our understanding of human consciousness and its potential capabilities. One of the primary challenges is the ongoing skepticism within the scientific community, which often views ESP research with suspicion due to the difficulty of reproducing results and the need for a widely accepted theoretical framework.

However, recent advances in technology and methodology offer new opportunities for investigating ESP. For example, neuroimaging techniques, such as functional magnetic resonance imaging (fMRI) and electroencephalography (EEG), allow researchers to explore the neural correlates of ESP experiences in real time. Similarly, quantum computing and artificial intelligence developments may provide new tools for analyzing complex datasets and identifying previously undetectable patterns.

Additionally, the growing interest in consciousness studies and the integration of Eastern and Western philosophical perspectives provide a fertile ground for exploring the potential of ESP. As researchers continue to push the boundaries of our understanding of consciousness, ESP may become an increasingly important area of inquiry, offering insights into the nature of reality, the mind, and the interconnectedness of all things.

2.17 Conclusion: The Ongoing Quest to Understand ESP

The study of ESP and telepathy represents one of the most challenging and intriguing areas of scientific inquiry. While these phenomena remain a subject of debate, the body of research—spanning over a century—suggests that there may be aspects of human cognition that conventional science has not yet fully understood.

As researchers continue exploring ESP's potential, integrating new technologies, interdisciplinary approaches, and emerging theories of consciousness will be crucial. The ongoing quest to understand ESP is not just about testing the limits of human perception but also about expanding our understanding of consciousness and its role in the fabric of reality.

The future of ESP continues to be an area where science meets mystery, with profound implications for our understanding of the mind, reality, and the potential capabilities of human consciousness.

3

PSYCHOKINESIS: MIND OVER MATTER

3.1 Introduction to Psychokinesis (PK)

Psychokinesis (PK), also known as telekinesis, refers to the purported ability of the mind to influence physical objects or events without any physical interaction. This phenomenon has been a subject of fascination and skepticism for centuries, appearing in various cultural myths and legends long before it became a topic of scientific inquiry. From ancient tales of sorcerers moving objects with a thought to modern depictions in popular media, PK has captured the imagination of people across the world.

In parapsychology, psychokinesis is studied as a potential manifestation of the mind's ability to affect matter directly. Researchers in the field aim to determine whether PK can be reliably demonstrated under controlled conditions and, if so, to understand the mechanisms that might underlie this mysterious phenomenon. While the evidence for PK remains controversial, it is a central topic in parapsychology due to its implications for our understanding of consciousness and the fundamental nature of reality.

In this chapter, we will explore the historical background of psychokinesis, review key experiments and findings, examine theoretical models that attempt to explain PK and consider the broader implications of this phenomenon for science and society. Through this exploration, we will address the challenges and controversies that have shaped the study of psychokinesis and assess its potential to expand our understanding of the mind's capabilities.

3.2 Historical Background and Case Studies

The concept of psychokinesis has a long history, with references to mind-over-matter abilities appearing in ancient texts and religious traditions. In many cultures, PK was attributed to supernatural beings, deities, or individuals with special spiritual or magical powers. These accounts often involved moving objects, controlling the elements, or even healing the sick through the power of thought alone.

In Western culture, one of the earliest references to psychokinesis can be found in the writings of **Plotinus**, a Greek philosopher who lived in the 3rd century AD. Plotinus suggested that the soul could influence the material world directly, a notion that aligns with the concept of PK. Similar ideas appeared in the works of later mystics and occultists, who claimed to be able to move objects or influence events through mental effort.

The modern study of psychokinesis began in the late 19th and early 20th centuries, alongside the rise of spiritualism and interest in paranormal phenomena. One of the most famous early cases involved **Nina Kulagina**, a Russian woman who gained international attention in the 1960s for her alleged ability to move small objects with her mind. Kulagina was filmed under controlled conditions, moving various objects, including matches, pendulums, and compass needles. While her demonstrations were widely publicized, they were also met with skepticism, with critics suggesting that hidden wires or other tricks could have produced the effects.

Another significant case in the history of psychokinesis is that of **Uri Geller**, an Israeli performer who became famous in the 1970s for his purported ability to bend spoons and keys using only his mind. Geller's performances were highly controversial, with some scientists supporting his claims while others accused him of fraud. Despite the debate surrounding Geller, his demonstrations brought PK to the forefront of public consciousness and inspired a wave of interest in psychokinesis research.

In the scientific community, J. B. Rhine systematically studied psychokinesis at Duke University in the 1930s and 1940s. In these experiments, Rhine used dice and asked participants to influence the outcome of the rolls through mental effort. While Rhine reported statistically significant results that suggested the presence of PK, his work was criticized for methodological flaws, including potential biases in the selection and interpretation of data. Nevertheless, Rhine's research laid the foundation for future studies of PK and remains a cornerstone in the history of parapsychology.

Throughout the 20th century, other researchers conducted PK experiments using various methods, including **random number generators (RNGs),** to test whether participants could influence the output of electronic devices. These studies produced mixed results, with some reporting significant effects and others finding no evidence of PK. The variability in findings has been an essential point of contention in the field, raising questions about the reliability and reproducibility of PK phenomena.

These historical case studies highlight the enduring interest in psychokinesis and the challenges of studying such a phenomenon scientifically. While the evidence for PK remains inconclusive, the cases of individuals like Nina Kulagina and Uri Geller and the early experiments by J. B. Rhine continue to spark debate and inspire further research into the mind's potential to influence matter.

3.3 Experimental Research in PK

Psychokinesis (PK), or the ability to influence objects or events with the mind, has been the subject of experimental research for nearly a century. These experiments aim to determine whether PK is a genuine phenomenon that can be measured and replicated under controlled conditions. Researchers have used various methods and technologies to investigate PK, with varying degrees of success.

Early PK Experiments: The earliest systematic studies of PK were conducted by J. B. Rhine at Duke University in the 1930s. Rhine's experiments primarily involved participants attempting to influence the outcome of dice rolls through mental effort. These experiments reported statistically significant results, suggesting that some individuals could influence physical objects with their minds. However, these findings were met with skepticism, mainly due to concerns about methodological rigor and the potential for biases in data interpretation.

Macro-PK vs. Micro-PK: PK research can be divided into macro-PK and micro-PK. Macro-PK refers to large-scale, observable effects, such as moving objects or bending metal. At the same time, micro-PK involves more subtle effects that are detectable only through statistical analysis, such as influencing random number generators (RNGs). While macro-PK claims are often sensationalized and difficult to verify, micro-PK research has gained more scientific attention due to its rigorous experimental protocols.

Random Number Generator (RNG) Studies: One of the most common methods used in micro-PK research involves RNGs. These devices generate sequences of numbers as close to being truly random as possible. In PK experiments, participants attempt to influence the output of RNGs to produce non-random patterns mentally. The results are then analyzed to determine whether the observed deviations from randomness are statistically significant. Some studies have reported significant results, suggesting that participants can influence RNGs, albeit with small effect sizes. However, these findings remain controversial, with critics arguing that the results could be due to subtle biases, methodological flaws, or even the statistical phenomena of regression to the mean.

PEAR Lab Experiments: One of the most well-known PK research programs was conducted at the Princeton Engineering Anomalies Research (PEAR) lab, which operated from 1979 to 2007.

The PEAR lab conducted extensive studies on micro-PK, primarily using RNGs and other electronic devices. Over nearly 30 years, the PEAR researchers collected a vast amount of data, which they claimed provided evidence for the existence of PK. However, the observed effects were generally small, and the broader scientific community met the findings skeptically. Critics argued that methodological issues could explain the PEAR results and that the small effect sizes reported did not provide compelling evidence for PK.

Meta-Analyses of PK Studies: To address the variability in PK research findings, several meta-analyses have been conducted, aggregating data from multiple studies to assess the overall evidence for PK. These meta-analyses have produced mixed results. Some have reported significant effects, suggesting that PK may be a natural phenomenon, while others have found no evidence for PK beyond what would be expected by chance. The inconsistency in findings has led to ongoing debates about the validity of PK research and the role of experimenter bias, publication bias, and methodological flaws in shaping the results.

Criticism and Replication Issues: A significant challenge in PK research is reproducing positive findings. Many experiments that initially report significant results fail to produce the same effects when repeated by independent researchers. This lack of replicability has been a central criticism of PK research, leading many scientists to question whether the phenomenon is natural or simply the result of statistical anomalies, biases, or experimental errors.

The Role of Consciousness: Despite these challenges, some researchers continue exploring the possibility that PK might be real and linked to the nature of consciousness itself. Theories have been proposed suggesting that consciousness may interact with the physical world in ways that are not yet understood by conventional science. These theories often draw on concepts from quantum mechanics, such as non-locality and entanglement, to propose that the mind may be able to influence matter at a fundamental level.

In conclusion, while experimental research into PK has produced intriguing results, the phenomenon remains controversial and needs to be better understood. The challenges of replicability, methodological rigor, and theoretical explanation continue to hinder the acceptance of PK within mainstream science. Nevertheless, PK research remains an important area of inquiry within parapsychology, as it raises fundamental questions about the nature of consciousness and the potential limits of human capability.

3.4 Micro-PK and Random Number Generators

Micro-PK, or micro-psychokinesis, refers to the subtle influence of the mind on small-scale systems, such as random number generators (RNGs). Unlike macro-PK, which involves visible effects like moving objects, micro-PK focuses on detecting minute deviations from expected outcomes in statistically random processes. This subtlety makes micro-PK particularly challenging to study, as it requires highly sensitive equipment and sophisticated statistical analysis to discern potential effects from noise.

Random Number Generator (RNG) Experiments: RNGs are devices that produce sequences of numbers that are expected to be random, meaning that each number in the sequence has an equal probability of occurring. In micro-PK experiments, participants attempt to influence the output of RNGs by mentally willing specific numbers to appear more frequently or by trying to induce patterns in otherwise random sequences.

The use of RNGs in PK research gained popularity in the 1960s and 1970s as computers became more widely available. Early experiments involved participants attempting to influence mechanical or electronic RNGs, such as dice rollers or electronic circuits. These studies produced mixed results, with some experiments reporting statistically significant deviations from randomness, while others found no evidence of PK.

PEAR Lab Studies: The Princeton Engineering Anomalies Research (PEAR) lab was a major center for RNG-based micro-PK research. Over nearly three decades, PEAR researchers conducted thousands of RNG experiments involving individual and group participants. Though statistically significant, the results showed only minor effects, leading to debates about their scientific validity. Critics of the PEAR findings argued that the small effect sizes could be attributed to methodological flaws, experimenter bias, or statistical artifacts rather than genuine PK.

Global Consciousness Project (GCP): Another notable RNG-based project is the Global Consciousness Project (GCP), which began in 1998. The GCP network consists of RNGs worldwide, continuously generating data. The project aims to detect correlations between global events (e.g., major disasters and significant political events) and deviations from expected randomness in the RNG data. Proponents of the GCP argue that the data shows subtle global consciousness effects, while critics point out that the results are subject to multiple comparisons and other statistical challenges.

Statistical Analysis in Micro-PK Research: Micro-PK research relies heavily on statistical methods to identify patterns or deviations in RNG output that could suggest a psychokinetic effect. Researchers typically use **p-values** to assess the statistical significance of their results, comparing the observed data against the null hypothesis of no PK effect. While some studies have reported p-values that suggest a deviation from randomness, the interpretation of these results is complicated by the **file drawer problem** and concerns about the robustness of the statistical techniques used.

Criticisms and Challenges: Micro-PK research faces several significant challenges. First, the small effect sizes reported in many studies raise questions about the practical significance of the findings. Even when statistically significant, these effects are often so small that they are difficult to distinguish from noise or experimental artifacts. Second, the replicability of micro-PK experiments remains a considerable concern. While some studies report positive results, many others fail to reproduce these findings, leading to ongoing debates about the reliability of the evidence.

Furthermore, the need for a theoretical model to explain how micro-PK could occur within the known laws of physics remains a significant hurdle. While some researchers have proposed that quantum mechanics might provide a framework for understanding PK, these ideas are speculative and have yet to be widely accepted within the scientific community.

In conclusion, micro-PK research, particularly studies involving RNGs, represents a rigorous attempt to test the limits of human consciousness and its potential influence on the physical world. Despite the challenges and criticisms, this line of research continues to intrigue scientists and laypeople alike, as it touches on fundamental questions about the nature of reality and the power of the mind.

3.5 Macro-PK: Large-Scale Phenomena

Macro-psychokinesis (macro-PK) refers to the ability to influence physical objects or events in ways that are visible to the naked eye. Unlike micro-PK, which involves subtle effects detectable only through statistical analysis, macro-PK involves large-scale phenomena, such as moving objects, bending metal, or affecting living organisms. These dramatic effects have captured the public imagination and have been the subject of scientific investigation and widespread skepticism.

Historical Context of Macro-PK: Claims of macro-PK have been part of human history for centuries, often associated with religious or mystical figures. Stories of saints, shamans, or spiritual leaders performing miraculous acts—such as levitation, healing, or controlling the elements—have been recorded in many cultures. While often anecdotal, these accounts have contributed to the enduring belief in the possibility of mind-over-matter phenomena.

Famous Macro-PK Cases: One of the most famous cases of alleged macro-PK is that of **Nina Kulagina**, a Russian woman who reportedly demonstrated the ability to move objects without touching them. Kulagina's demonstrations, filmed and observed by Soviet scientists, included moving small items like matches and turning compass needles. While these feats were impressive, they were also controversial, with skeptics arguing that they could be explained by sleight of hand or other tricks.

Another well-known figure associated with macro-PK is **Uri Geller**, an Israeli performer famous in the 1970s for his purported ability to bend spoons and keys with his mind. Geller's performances were televised and became a cultural phenomenon but also attracted significant skepticism. Magicians and skeptics, including James Randi, demonstrated how Geller's feats could be replicated using simple tricks, leading to debates over whether Geller possessed genuine psychic abilities or was simply a skilled illusionist.

Laboratory Investigations of Macro-PK: Despite the public fascination with macro-PK, scientific investigations into these phenomena have been challenging. One of the main difficulties is the need for more **reliable replication** under controlled conditions. Many claims of macro-PK have been made in informal or unscientific settings, where the possibility of fraud or error cannot be ruled out. In the laboratory, where strict controls are in place to prevent deception, macro-PK effects have been much more challenging to demonstrate.

Some researchers have attempted to study macro-PK using metal bending experiments, where participants are asked to bend metal objects, such as spoons or rods, through mental effort. While a few studies have reported positive results, these findings have been met with skepticism, as the effects could be explained by physical force applied to the objects. The challenge of ensuring that no physical contact occurs during these experiments has made it difficult to draw definitive conclusions about the reality of macro-PK.

Criticism and Controversy: The study of macro-PK has been plagued by controversy, mainly due to the difficulty of ruling out alternative explanations, such as trickery or wishful thinking. The dramatic nature of macro-PK claims makes them appealing to the public and vulnerable to charlatan exploitation. This has led to a widespread perception of macro-PK as a pseudoscientific phenomenon despite the efforts of some researchers to investigate it seriously.

The Role of Belief and Expectation: An intriguing aspect of macro-PK research is the role of belief and expectation in shaping both the outcomes of experiments and the public's perception of the phenomenon. Some studies have suggested that participants who strongly believe in their ability to influence objects may be more likely to report successful PK experiences. This raises the question of whether macro-PK is a genuine phenomenon or a psychological effect driven by expectation and suggestion.

Theoretical Considerations: Theoretical explanations for macro-PK are even more elusive than those for micro-PK. While some researchers have attempted to link PK with quantum mechanics or other physical theories, these explanations remain speculative and have yet to be widely accepted within the scientific community. The lack of a plausible mechanism for how the mind could produce large-scale physical effects without physical interaction remains a significant barrier to macro-PK acceptance.

In conclusion, while macro-PK continues to capture the imagination, its status as a scientifically verified phenomenon remains highly questionable. The difficulties in replicating macro-PK effects under controlled conditions, the potential for fraud, and the lack of a theoretical framework have led many scientists to view macro-PK skeptically. However, the study of macro-PK remains an area of interest within parapsychology, as it raises fundamental questions about the nature of reality and the limits of human potential.

3.6 Theories and Mechanisms of Psychokinesis

One of the most significant challenges in PK research is the need for a widely accepted theoretical framework that can explain how the mind might influence matter. Several hypotheses have been proposed, drawing on concepts from quantum physics, consciousness studies, and parapsychology.

One of the more widely discussed theories is that PK might involve quantum interactions, where the observer (in this case, the person attempting PK) influences the outcome of a quantum process. This idea is loosely based on the observer effect in quantum mechanics, where the act of observation affects the state of a quantum system. Some researchers have speculated that consciousness might similarly influence physical systems, although this idea remains speculative and controversial (Radin, 2006).

Another hypothesis revolves around "intention," where focused mental intention can change physical reality. Researchers like William Tiller have explored this idea, conducting experiments to test whether human intention can influence physical systems, such as water structure or biological organisms' growth. While these studies have produced intriguing results, they have also been criticized for methodological weaknesses and difficulty replicating findings (Tiller et al., 2001).

A more radical hypothesis is that PK might involve a non-local aspect of consciousness, where the mind is not confined to the brain but can interact with distant physical systems through mechanisms not yet understood by conventional science. This idea aligns with some quantum mechanics interpretations, suggesting that entanglement and non-locality might allow for connections between distant objects or systems. However, these ideas remain speculative and are still mainly on the fringes of mainstream scientific discourse (Goswami, 1993).

3.7 Challenges and Controversies in PK Research

The study of psychokinesis (PK) presents significant challenges and has sparked considerable controversy, reflecting the phenomenon's complexity and ambiguity. These issues range from methodological concerns to broader philosophical and scientific debates.

Methodological Issues: One of the foremost challenges in PK research is designing experiments that can definitively demonstrate the phenomenon. Due to the subtle and often unpredictable nature of PK effects, capturing them in a controlled environment is challenging. For example, J. B. Rhine's early experiments on PK using dice rolls were criticized for potential methodological flaws, including inadequate controls and possible bias (Rhine, 1947). Modern researchers have sought to mitigate these concerns by employing double-blind protocols and automated data collection systems, but challenges remain (Kennedy, 2004).

Replicability Problems: The ability to replicate findings consistently across different studies is crucial in science, yet PK experiments often struggle with replicability. Many initial studies report positive results not reproduced by independent researchers or under different conditions (Hyman, 1989). This raises skepticism about PK research's reliability, leading some critics to argue that positive results might be due to experimental artifacts, biases, or statistical anomalies rather than genuine PK effects (Alcock, 2003).

Experimenter Bias: Experimenter bias is another primary concern in PK research. The expectations and beliefs of the experimenter can unconsciously influence the outcomes, a problem highlighted in various studies. For instance, Rosenthal (1976) discusses how even subtle cues or variations in experimental conditions can skew results. To address this, double-blind procedures have been implemented to reduce bias, where neither the experimenter nor the participant knows the specific conditions being tested. However, these measures do not eliminate the risk of bias, particularly in experiments involving subtle PK effects (Hyman & Honorton, 1986).

The File Drawer Problem: The file drawer problem refers to the tendency for studies with null results to remain unpublished, leading to a skewed perception of the evidence in favor of PK (Rosenthal, 1979). This issue is particularly relevant in PK research, where the pressure to produce positive results can lead to selective reporting. Meta-analyses attempt to correct this by including published and unpublished studies, but the file drawer problem remains a significant concern (Bösch et al., 2006).

Skepticism from the Broader Scientific Community: The lack of a widely accepted theoretical framework to explain how PK could occur has contributed to skepticism within the scientific community. Most current models of the physical world do not account for the possibility that the mind can directly influence matter without any physical intermediary. This theoretical gap has led many scientists to view PK as incompatible with established scientific principles

(Hyman, 1989). The association of PK with paranormal phenomena and its frequent portrayal in popular culture as a form of "magic" further undermines its credibility (Randi, 1982).

Fraud and Deception: The history of PK research has been tainted by fraud and deception, particularly in cases involving dramatic macro-PK effects. High-profile cases of fraudulent mediums and psychics who claimed to demonstrate PK have cast a long shadow over the field. The potential for deception remains a concern in modern research, especially in experiments that are not tightly controlled (Hyman, 1985). Despite rigorous scientific standards, the possibility of fraud remains a significant issue researchers must address (Randi, 1982).

Philosophical Implications: PK research also raises profound philosophical questions. If PK were proven to be real, it would challenge the materialist paradigm that underpins much of modern science, suggesting that the mind has capabilities that extend beyond the physical brain (Chalmers, 1996). This possibility has significant implications for our understanding of consciousness, free will, and the nature of reality itself. However, these philosophical implications also contribute to the controversy surrounding PK, as they require a fundamental rethinking of long-held assumptions about the world (Laszlo, 2004).

In conclusion, PK research is fraught with challenges, from methodological issues to deep philosophical questions. While some researchers continue to explore PK as a genuine aspect of human consciousness, the field remains contentious and is often viewed skeptically. The future of PK research will depend on developing new methodologies, producing replicable results, and integrating PK into a broader scientific framework that can accommodate its potential implications.

3.8 Applications of Psychokinesis

Exploring psychokinesis (PK) extends beyond theoretical inquiry and considers potential applications in various fields. If PK were proven to be a genuine and reliable phenomenon, it could revolutionize numerous areas of human activity. However, the PK's speculative nature means that these applications remain largely hypothetical.

Medical Applications: One of the most intriguing potential applications of PK is in medicine. If individuals could influence their own or others' physical health through PK, it could lead to new forms of treatment and healing. For example, PK could potentially be used to promote tissue regeneration, control pain, or even target specific cells in the body to treat diseases such as cancer. Some researchers have drawn parallels between PK and the placebo effect, suggesting that the mind's ability to influence the body could be harnessed in new ways (Sheldrake, 2012).

Military and Defense: The potential military applications of PK have been a subject of interest, particularly during the Cold War. Both the United States and the Soviet Union conducted research into psychic phenomena, including PK, as part of their broader efforts to develop new intelligence and defense capabilities. For instance, the U.S. government's Stargate Project investigated the potential use of PK and other psychic abilities for espionage and military operations (May 1996). While these programs were eventually discontinued, using PK in military contexts remains a point of discussion in speculative literature.

Psychokinesis in Technology: PK could be applied to human-computer interaction, allowing individuals to control machines or devices with their minds. This concept, often explored in science fiction, would involve using PK to manipulate computer systems, operate machinery, or interface with artificial intelligence directly. Such technology could have significant implications for accessibility, enabling people with disabilities to interact with the world in new and empowering ways (Radin, 2006).

Environmental Manipulation: Another potential application of PK involves environmental control. If PK could be harnessed to influence weather patterns or geological processes, it could be used for disaster prevention or environmental management. For example, PK could dissipate storms, prevent earthquakes, or control wildfires.

However, this application is highly speculative and would require a far greater understanding of PK than currently exists (Radin, 1997).

Ethical Considerations: The potential applications of PK also raise significant ethical questions. The ability to influence physical objects or events with the mind could be used for beneficial and harmful purposes. For instance, while PK could be employed for healing or environmental management, it could also be weaponized or used for manipulation and control. This dual-use potential means that any development of PK applications must be carefully regulated, with strict ethical guidelines in place (Stapp, 2009).

Personal Development and Spiritual Growth: Beyond practical applications, PK could also have implications for personal development and spiritual growth. Some proponents of PK suggest that developing this ability could lead to a deeper understanding of the mind and consciousness and greater control over one's thoughts and emotions. In this sense, PK could be viewed as a physical phenomenon and a tool for personal transformation and self-realization (Tart, 2009).

In conclusion, while the potential applications of PK are fascinating, they remain largely theoretical due to the ongoing debate about the phenomenon's reality. If PK were proven authentic and reliable, it could have far-reaching implications for medicine, technology, environmental management, and military strategy. However, these possibilities also highlight the need for careful ethical consideration and regulation to ensure that PK is used responsibly and for the benefit of humanity.

3.9 Future Directions in PK Research

As psychokinesis (PK) continues to be a subject of scientific inquiry and debate, the future of PK research hinges on several key developments. These include technological advancements, interdisciplinary collaboration, and integration of new theoretical frameworks.

Technological Advancements: Emerging technologies, such as more sophisticated random number generators (RNGs), enhanced brain imaging techniques, and advanced data analysis methods, could provide more precise measurements and potentially unveil subtle PK effects that have eluded detection in previous studies. For example, improvements in EEG and fMRI technology could allow researchers to understand PK's neural correlates better, potentially linking specific brain states to psychokinetic activity (Radin, 2006).

Interdisciplinary Collaboration: Future PK research may benefit from closer collaboration between disciplines, including physics, neuroscience, psychology, and parapsychology. By integrating insights from quantum mechanics, cognitive science, and consciousness studies, researchers could develop more robust theoretical models that explain how PK might operate within the laws of physics. Such interdisciplinary efforts could also help to refine experimental protocols and reduce the influence of biases and artifacts (Stapp, 2009).

Exploration of Non-Western Perspectives: Expanding PK research to include non-Western perspectives and methodologies could provide new insights and broaden the field's scope. Many cultures have traditions and practices that involve mind-over-matter phenomena, and incorporating these into scientific inquiry could lead to novel approaches and potentially corroborative evidence (Tart, 2009).

Public Perception and Media Influence: The way PK research is presented to the public and in the media will also play a crucial role in shaping the future of the field. Public interest in PK has often been driven by sensationalist media portrayals, which can undermine the credibility of serious scientific research. Moving forward, researchers must find ways to communicate their findings responsibly and accurately to foster a more informed and balanced public discourse (Randi, 1982).

Ethical and Societal Considerations: As PK research progresses, it will be essential to consider the ethical implications of potential applications. Developing ethical guidelines for PK experimentation and application will be crucial, particularly if the phenomenon proves to be real and capable of being harnessed for practical purposes. Addressing societal concerns about privacy, consent, and the potential misuse of PK will be necessary to ensure that advancements in this field are used responsibly (Sheldrake, 2012).

Integration with Consciousness Studies: As research into consciousness continues to evolve, PK may be increasingly studied within the broader context of consciousness exploration. The possibility that PK is connected to fundamental aspects of consciousness, such as intentionality or the nature of reality, suggests that future PK research could contribute to a deeper understanding of consciousness itself. This integration could also lead to new theoretical models that bridge the gap between parapsychology and mainstream science (Chalmers, 1996).

In conclusion, the future of PK research is likely to be shaped by technological advancements, interdisciplinary collaboration, and the exploration of new theoretical frameworks. By addressing the challenges that have historically plagued the field and incorporating new perspectives, PK research may eventually provide clearer answers about the potential of the mind to influence the physical world.

3.10 PK and Consciousness Studies

The relationship between psychokinesis (PK) and consciousness has long intrigued researchers. PK challenges our understanding of consciousness by suggesting that the mind might exert influence over physical matter, potentially pointing to a deeper connection between consciousness and the fabric of reality itself.

PK as a Manifestation of Consciousness: Some researchers propose that PK could be a direct manifestation of the mind's influence on the physical world, implying that consciousness is not merely a passive observer but an active participant in shaping reality (Stapp, 2009). This idea aligns with certain interpretations of quantum mechanics, where the observer is thought to play a crucial role in determining outcomes at the quantum level (Radin, 2006).

Non-local Consciousness: The concept of non-local consciousness is another area where PK and consciousness studies intersect.

Non-locality, a term borrowed from quantum physics, refers to the idea that objects or events can be correlated across distances without any direct connection. In the context of consciousness, non-locality suggests that the mind may not be confined to the brain or body but could extend beyond these boundaries, potentially allowing for phenomena like PK (Tart, 2009).

Mind-Matter Interaction Models: Theories such as the mind-matter interaction model propose that consciousness fundamentally influences physical processes. These models suggest that PK might be understood as a natural extension of consciousness, capable of interacting with and altering the physical world (Sheldrake, 2012). This view challenges the traditional materialist perspective, which holds that consciousness is merely a byproduct of brain activity without directly influencing the physical realm.

Experimental Evidence and Consciousness: Experiments in PK often involve measuring the influence of intention, an essential aspect of consciousness, on physical systems such as random number generators. While the results have been mixed, with some studies showing significant effects and others failing to replicate them, the ongoing research continues to explore the possibility that consciousness could play an active role in shaping physical reality (Bösch, Steinkamp, & Boller, 2006).

Implications for the Study of Consciousness: If PK is real, it would imply that consciousness has properties and capabilities that science does not currently understand. This could lead to a radical rethinking of the mind's relationship to the body and the environment, and it would challenge the prevailing materialist paradigm that dominates neuroscience and psychology (Chalmers, 1996). Understanding PK could thus provide new insights into the nature of consciousness, free will, and the mind's potential.

In conclusion, the study of PK offers a unique perspective on consciousness, suggesting that the mind may have a more active and expansive role in the universe than traditionally believed. Future research into PK, particularly concerning consciousness studies, may lead to groundbreaking discoveries that reshape our understanding of reality.

3.11 The Philosophical Implications of PK

If proven, the phenomenon of psychokinesis (PK) would have profound philosophical implications that challenge many of the foundational assumptions of modern science and philosophy. These implications touch on the nature of reality, the mind-body problem, and the limits of human potential.

Challenging Materialism: One of PK's most significant philosophical challenges is its incompatibility with materialism, the dominant paradigm in modern science. Materialism holds that all phenomena, including consciousness, can be explained through physical processes. PK, however, suggests that the mind can directly influence matter, which contradicts the materialist view that the mind is a product of physical brain activity and cannot affect the physical world independently (Chalmers, 1996). If PK were accepted as genuine, it would necessitate a revision of materialist assumptions and potentially lead to developing a new, more inclusive framework for understanding reality.

The Mind-Body Problem: PK also directly engages with the mind-body problem, a central issue in philosophy concerning the relationship between the mind and the physical body. Traditional dualism, as proposed by René Descartes, posits that the mind and body are separate substances that interact in some way. If confirmed, PK would provide evidence for the mind's ability to interact with the physical world in ways not accounted for by current scientific understanding. This would support dualist or other non-materialist theories of mind, suggesting that consciousness might have a degree of independence from the brain and could interact with the physical world in ways that are not fully understood (Tart, 2009).

Implications for Free Will: The existence of PK could also have implications for the concept of free will. If the mind can influence physical objects or events, this suggests that human beings have more control over their environment and circumstances than is typically assumed. This could support libertarian views of free will, which argue that individuals have genuine choice and control over their actions, as opposed to deterministic views, which hold that all events are predetermined by prior causes (Stapp, 2009). PK might be seen as a manifestation of free will, demonstrating the mind's ability to change the physical world.

The Nature of Reality: The reality of PK would also raise questions about the fundamental nature of reality. If the mind can influence matter, reality might be more malleable and interconnected than previously thought. This could support holistic or panpsychist views, which propose that consciousness is a fundamental aspect of reality and that all parts of the universe are interconnected in a way that allows for mind-matter interaction (Sheldrake, 2012). Such views challenge the traditional scientific view of the universe as composed of discrete, independently functioning parts and instead suggest that reality might be a more unified, dynamic system.

Ethical Implications: The potential for PK to be harnessed for practical purposes also raises significant ethical questions. If individuals could influence their environment or others through PK, this would necessitate new ethical guidelines to ensure that such abilities are used responsibly. Consent, privacy, and the potential for misuse must be carefully considered. Additionally, the existence of PK could challenge our understanding of moral responsibility, mainly if individuals can influence outcomes in ways that are not immediately apparent to others (Stapp, 2009).

Integrating PK into a New Scientific Paradigm: If PK were accepted as a genuine phenomenon, it would require the development of a new scientific paradigm that can account for mind-matter interactions. This would likely involve a synthesis of insights from quantum mechanics, consciousness studies, and traditional metaphysical theories, resulting in a more comprehensive understanding of the universe and the role of consciousness within it (Radin, 2006).

In conclusion, PK's philosophical implications are profound, challenging many of the foundational assumptions of modern science and philosophy. If PK were proven to be real, it would necessitate a radical rethinking of the nature of reality, the mind-body relationship, and the limits of human potential.

3.12 The Role of PK in Cultural and Religious Traditions

Psychokinesis (PK), or the ability to influence physical objects with the mind, has been a part of human culture and religious traditions for centuries. Across different cultures, PK has often been associated with spiritual or supernatural powers, and these beliefs have shaped how PK is perceived and understood in various societies.

PK in Ancient Cultures: In many ancient cultures, PK-like abilities were attributed to gods, spirits, or individuals with special spiritual status, such as shamans or priests. For example, in ancient Egypt, the pharaohs were believed to possess divine powers, including the ability to control the elements or move objects with their will. Similarly, in Hinduism, certain yogis and sages are said to have mastered siddhis—supernatural powers that include levitation and the ability to influence matter with the mind (Feuerstein, 1998).

PK in Religious Miracles: PK is also a common theme in religious miracles. In Christianity, saints and mystics are often depicted as able to perform miraculous acts, such as moving objects, healing the sick, or levitating through divine intervention or the power of faith. These accounts are evidence of the divine working through human intermediaries and have been essential to religious narratives throughout history (Thurston, 1952).

Shamanic Traditions: In shamanic traditions, particularly those of indigenous cultures in Asia, Africa, and the Americas, shamans are believed to interact with the spirit world and use their mental and spiritual powers to influence the physical world. This includes PK-like abilities, such as moving objects, controlling weather, or healing through ritualistic practices. These abilities are often seen as gifts from the spirits or as the result of rigorous spiritual training (Eliade, 1964).

PK in Eastern Philosophies: In Eastern philosophies, particularly in Buddhism and Taoism, the concept of mind over matter is integral to understanding the universe and the self. In Buddhism, deep meditation and mental discipline are believed to unlock supernatural abilities, including PK, as one progresses toward enlightenment. In Taoism, the concept of qi (life force) is a subtle energy that can be harnessed and directed by the mind, leading to PK-like phenomena (Wong, 2002).

Modern Spiritual Movements: In the modern era, PK has been embraced by various spiritual movements, particularly within the New Age community. PK is often linked to concepts of personal empowerment and the idea that individuals can manifest their reality through focused intention and belief. This perspective is reflected in practices such as the law of attraction, where believers assert that positive thoughts and intentions can bring about positive changes in the physical world (Heelas, 1996).

PK and Skepticism in Culture: While PK has been celebrated in many cultural and religious contexts, it has also been met with skepticism, particularly in the scientific and secular communities. This skepticism has often been fueled by the association of PK with fraud, superstition, and the paranormal. As a result, PK remains a contentious topic, with its acceptance varying widely across different cultural and religious landscapes (Randi, 1982).

In conclusion, PK has played a significant role in cultural and religious traditions throughout history, often viewed as a manifestation of spiritual power or divine intervention. While the phenomenon continues to captivate and inspire, it also faces challenges from scientific skepticism, making it a complex and multifaceted topic that bridges the realms of spirituality, culture, and science.

3.13 PK in Modern Media and Pop Culture

Psychokinesis (PK) has long captivated the imagination of storytellers and audiences alike, making it a prominent theme in modern media and pop culture. From comic books and films to television series and video games, PK is often depicted as a powerful and mysterious ability that allows characters to manipulate objects, people, and even entire environments with their minds.

PK in Superhero Media: One of the most common portrayals of PK is found in superhero comics and films, where characters with telekinetic abilities can move objects, fly, or create energy shields. Iconic characters like Jean Grey from the *X-Men* series and Eleven from *Stranger Things* showcase these powers, often using them in dramatic, high-stakes scenarios. These depictions typically emphasize the power and danger of PK, often linking it to themes of control, power, and the burden of extraordinary abilities (Friedman, 2017).

PK in Horror and Science Fiction: PK also appears frequently in horror and science fiction genres, often associated with the paranormal or extraterrestrial beings. In Stephen King's novel *Carrie*, the titular character's PK abilities are triggered by extreme emotional distress, leading to catastrophic consequences. Similarly, in the film *Chronicle*, three teenagers develop PK powers after encountering a mysterious object, ultimately exploring the ethical dilemmas and personal conflicts that arise from such abilities (King, 1974; Landis, 2012).

Video Games and Interactive Media: Video games have embraced PK as a gameplay mechanic, allowing players to use telekinetic powers to solve puzzles, combat enemies, or manipulate the environment. Games like *Control* and *Psi-Ops: The Mindgate Conspiracy* let players experiment with PK in immersive, interactive settings, often blending action with narrative elements that explore the origins and implications of these powers (Remedy Entertainment, 2019).

PK as a Metaphor: Beyond entertainment, PK is often used as a metaphor for the power of the mind and the potential for humans to transcend physical limitations. This theme resonates with audiences drawn to stories of self-discovery, personal empowerment, and the exploration of human potential. In many cases, PK serves as a narrative device to explore more profound philosophical questions about the nature of reality, the mind-body connection, and the boundaries of human capability (Friedman, 2017).

Public Perception and Skepticism: While PK is popular in the media, its portrayal often blurs the line between fiction and reality, leading to public fascination and skepticism. Media representations can perpetuate misconceptions about PK, presenting it as an unquestioned fact or an impossible fantasy. This duality reflects broader societal attitudes toward paranormal phenomena, where belief and skepticism coexist, influenced by popular culture and scientific discourse (Randi, 1982).

In conclusion, PK remains a compelling and versatile theme in modern media and pop culture, serving as both an exciting narrative element and a metaphor for human potential. Its portrayals in various forms of entertainment continue to shape public perceptions of PK, blending fiction with the enduring mystery of the mind's capabilities.

4

REMOTE VIEWING

4.1 Introduction to Remote Viewing

Remote viewing (RV) is a practice that claims to enable individuals to perceive distant or unseen targets using extrasensory perception (ESP). Unlike traditional psychic abilities, RV is often described as a learned skill that can be developed and honed through training. The concept gained significant attention during the Cold War, mainly through government-sponsored programs exploring its potential applications in intelligence gathering and military operations.

Remote viewing has been the subject of both scientific investigation and widespread interest. While many in the scientific community remain skeptical of its claims, proponents argue that RV offers evidence of the mind's ability to transcend space and time. This chapter will explore the history, methodologies, and controversies surrounding remote viewing and its implications for our understanding of consciousness.

4.2 The Origins of Remote Viewing

The concept of remote viewing can be traced back to ancient times, with practices akin to RV found in various cultures and religious traditions. In ancient Greece, the Oracle of Delphi was believed to possess the ability to perceive distant events and guide those who sought her counsel. Similarly, shamanic practices worldwide have long involved rituals to gain insight into distant places or future events (Eliade, 1964).

In the modern era, the scientific investigation of remote viewing began in earnest during the 20th century. The term "remote viewing" was popularized in the 1970s through the work of physicists Russell Targ and Harold Puthoff at the Stanford Research Institute (SRI). Their experiments aimed to test whether individuals could accurately describe remote locations or objects without prior knowledge of the target. The results of these experiments were controversial, with some claiming significant success and others criticizing the methodologies used (Targ & Puthoff, 1977).

The U.S. government became particularly interested in RV during the Cold War, leading to the establishment of the Stargate Project. This program sought to explore RV's potential for military and intelligence applications, with mixed results. While some remote viewers reportedly provided helpful intelligence, the program's overall efficacy remains a topic of debate (May 1996).

4.3 Methodologies and Protocols of Remote Viewing

Remote viewing is typically conducted under controlled conditions designed to minimize the influence of external cues and biases. A standard RV session involves a "viewer" who attempts to describe a target—such as a location, object, or event- based solely on their mental impressions. The viewer is often provided minimal information, such as a set of coordinates or a vague descriptor, to prevent them from relying on prior knowledge or logical deduction.

The protocols for RV have been refined over the years to increase the reliability and validity of the results. The **Coordinate Remote Viewing (CRV)** method, developed by Ingo Swann, is one of the most well-known approaches. CRV involves a structured process in which the viewer records their impressions in stages, moving from general sensory impressions to more specific details. This method is designed to help the viewer access subconscious information without interference from their conscious mind (Swann, 1996).

Another important aspect of RV is **double-blind protocols**, where both the viewer and the monitor (the person guiding the session) are unaware of the target's identity. This helps to prevent any inadvertent influence on the viewer's perceptions and enhances the credibility of the results. Despite these precautions, the subjective nature of RV and the difficulty in objectively verifying the accuracy of the impressions remain significant challenges (Radin, 1997).

4.4 Key Experiments and Findings

Throughout the history of remote viewing research, several vital experiments have shaped the field and contributed to ongoing debates about its validity. One of the most famous early studies was conducted by Targ and Puthoff at SRI, where participants were asked to describe remote locations unknown to them. The results, published in Nature, suggested that some participants could produce accurate descriptions, leading to widespread interest in RV (Targ & Puthoff, 1977).

Another significant study was the **Army's Project Stargate**, which ran from the 1970s to the 1990s. This classified program used remote viewers to gather intelligence on military and geopolitical targets. While some reports claimed that remote viewers provided valuable information, the program's overall success remains disputed, with many critics arguing that the results were inconsistent and lacked rigorous scientific validation (May 1996).

More recent studies have continued to explore RV's potential, often focusing on refining methodologies and addressing previous criticisms. For example, experiments conducted at the **Princeton**

Engineering Anomalies Research (PEAR) laboratory aimed to assess the accuracy of remote viewing under highly controlled conditions. While some positive results were reported, the effects observed were generally minor, and the findings have been met with skepticism (Jahn & Dunne, 2005).

4.5 Applications and Implications of Remote Viewing

Remote viewing has been explored for various practical applications, particularly in intelligence and military operations. During the Cold War, the U.S. government invested significant resources into studying RV as a potential tool for espionage, with mixed results. While some remote viewers reportedly provided valuable intelligence, others produced inaccurate or ambiguous information, leading to debates about the reliability of RV as a practical tool (May 1996).

Beyond military and intelligence applications, remote viewing has also been investigated for its potential in other areas, such as archaeology, search and rescue operations, and personal development. For example, some researchers have used RV to locate ancient ruins or lost artifacts, while others have explored its potential for enhancing creativity and problem-solving abilities (Radin, 1997).

The implications of RV extend beyond its practical applications, touching on broader questions about the nature of consciousness and the mind's ability to access information beyond space and time constraints. Suppose remote viewing is validated as a genuine phenomenon. In that case, it will challenge current scientific models of perception and cognition, suggesting that the mind may have capabilities that are not yet fully understood (Targ, 2012).

4.6 Criticisms and Skepticism

Remote viewing has been the subject of significant criticism and skepticism from the scientific community. Critics argue that many RV experiments suffer from methodological flaws, such as inadequate controls, the potential for sensory leakage, and the reliance on subjective interpretations of results. These issues, they argue, make it difficult to determine whether the observed effects are genuinely due to RV or are the result of chance, suggestion, or other psychological factors (Hyman, 1985).

Another common criticism is the need for replicability in RV studies. While some experiments have reported positive results, others must reproduce these findings under similar conditions. This inconsistency has led many scientists to question the validity of RV as a reliable and reproducible phenomenon (Hyman, 1989).

Despite these criticisms, RV proponents argue that the phenomenon cannot be dismissed outright and that further research is needed to understand its potential and limitations fully. They point to double-blind protocols, improved methodologies, and the accumulation of anecdotal evidence as reasons to continue exploring RV as a legitimate area of inquiry (Radin, 1997).

4.7 Ethical and Philosophical Considerations

The study of remote viewing raises important ethical and philosophical questions, particularly regarding the implications of RV for our understanding of consciousness, privacy, and human potential. If RV is actual, it could challenge traditional notions of space, time, and the boundaries of the mind, leading to a re-evaluation of how we understand perception and knowledge (Tart, 2009).

One of the primary ethical concerns with RV is the potential invasion of privacy. If individuals can access information about distant locations or events without physical presence, it raises questions about the right to privacy and the potential to misuse such abilities. Safeguards would need to be established to prevent the unethical use of RV, particularly in sensitive areas such as personal relationships or national security (May 1996).

From a philosophical perspective, RV challenges the materialist paradigm that underlies much of modern science. If the mind can access information beyond the limits of the senses, it suggests that consciousness may not be confined to the brain or bound by the physical laws that govern the material world. This could have profound implications for our understanding of reality and the nature of human experience (Chalmers, 1996).

4.8 Case Studies and Anecdotal Evidence

Remote viewing (RV) is supported by experimental research, anecdotal evidence, and case studies. These accounts often describe instances where individuals have used RV to locate lost objects, solve crimes, or gain insights into distant locations or future events. While anecdotal evidence lacks the rigor of controlled experiments, it provides a valuable perspective on how RV has been applied in real-world situations.

The Pat Price Case: One of the most famous remote viewers was Pat Price, a former police officer who became involved in the U.S. government's Stargate Project. Price reportedly provided highly accurate descriptions of secret military installations, including details later confirmed by reconnaissance missions. His work was so impressive that it led to further investment in RV research by U.S. intelligence agencies (McMoneagle, 2002).

The "Nine-Digit Zip Code" Case: Another well-known case involves a remote viewer tasked with identifying a target based only on a nine-digit zip code. The viewer described a remote island in Alaska and accurately pinpointed the features of a top-secret facility. The accuracy of this session was later confirmed through classified intelligence sources, further demonstrating the potential of RV in intelligence work (Targ, 2012).

Locating Hostages: Anecdotal evidence also includes cases where RV was used in attempts to locate hostages or missing persons. For example, in the 1980s, remote viewers were involved in efforts to find U.S. hostages in Iran. While the results were mixed, some descriptions provided by the remote viewers were reportedly accurate enough to be applicable to intelligence agencies (May 1996).

Archaeological Discoveries: Remote viewing has also been applied in archaeology. For instance, RV practitioners have claimed success in locating ancient ruins and artifacts that were previously unknown. Although these claims are often difficult to verify, they contribute to the narrative that RV may have practical applications beyond intelligence gathering (Radin, 1997).

Personal Anecdotes: Beyond high-profile cases, many individuals have reported using RVs in their personal lives, such as finding lost items or gaining insights into personal dilemmas. These stories are typically shared within RV communities and contribute to the belief that RVs are a skill that can be developed and used by anyone with proper training (Swann, 1996).

Skeptical Perspective on Anecdotal Evidence: While these stories are compelling, skeptics argue that anecdotal evidence is inherently unreliable due to the lack of control over variables and the potential for confirmation bias. They contend that many of these accounts could be explained by coincidence, logical deduction, or even subconscious memories rather than actual remote viewing (Hyman, 1989).

In conclusion, while anecdotal evidence and case studies provide intriguing examples of remote viewing in action, they also highlight the need for rigorous scientific validation. These accounts offer valuable insights but must be carefully weighed against the challenges of verifying and replicating such experiences.

4.9 Remote Viewing in the Modern Era

Recently, interest in remote viewing (RV) has grown, driven by scientific curiosity and popular fascination. The development of new technologies, the expansion of online communities, and the ongoing exploration of consciousness have all contributed to the resurgence of RV as a subject of study and practice.

Technological Advances and RV: The rise of the internet and digital communication has made it easier for individuals to learn about and practice remote viewing. Online courses, webinars, and forums have proliferated, offering training and guidance to those interested in developing their RV abilities. These platforms allow for sharing experiences, techniques, and feedback, creating a global community of remote viewers who can collaborate and support one another (Brown, 2010).

Moreover, brain imaging and neurotechnology advancements have opened new avenues for studying RV. Researchers can now observe brain activity in real-time during RV sessions, potentially identifying neural correlates of the experience. These technologies may help to elucidate the mechanisms underlying RV and provide empirical support for the phenomenon (Radin, 2006).

Remote Viewing in Popular Culture: Remote viewing has also maintained a presence in popular culture, appearing in films, television shows, and literature. The portrayal of RV in media often blends elements of science fiction, mysticism, and espionage, contributing to its mystique. For example, the 2009 film *The Men Who Stare at Goats* popularized the idea of government-sponsored psychic programs, including RV, albeit in a satirical context (Ronson, 2004).

These cultural depictions have helped to sustain public interest in RV, even as scientific debates continue. While such portrayals can sometimes lead to misunderstandings about RV's nature, they also keep the concept in the public consciousness, inspiring new generations to explore its possibilities.

Integration with Consciousness Studies: The study of RV is increasingly being integrated into broader research on consciousness. As scientists continue to explore the nature of consciousness and its potential non-local aspects, RV is seen as a valuable case study that may shed light on how the mind interacts with the world. This interdisciplinary approach could help to bridge the gap between traditional scientific paradigms and the experiential aspects of RV, leading to a more comprehensive understanding of both (Tart, 2009).

Ongoing Challenges and Controversies: Despite the continued interest in RV, many challenges and controversies that have historically plagued the field remain. The lack of consistent, replicable results continues to be a significant hurdle, as does the skepticism of the broader scientific community. Additionally, the subjective nature of RV experiences makes establishing objective criteria for success complex, further complicating efforts to validate the phenomenon (Hyman, 1989).

Despite ongoing challenges, remote viewing has found new life in the modern era. One significant development has been the increasing accessibility of RV training and practice, primarily driven by the Internet. Today, aspiring remote viewers can access online courses, participate in virtual RV sessions, and engage with a global community of enthusiasts. These developments have democratized RV, allowing more people to explore and develop this ability (Brown, 2010).

Additionally, the integration of RV into broader consciousness studies has opened new avenues for research. As scientists seek to understand the nature of consciousness, RV is often studied alongside other phenomena like lucid dreaming, out-of-body experiences, and meditation. This interdisciplinary approach is gradually shifting the perception of RV from a fringe pursuit to a legitimate area of inquiry within the study of human potential (Tart, 2009).

Popular culture also continues to play a role in keeping RV in the public eye. Films, TV shows, and literature frequently depict RV in various forms, blending science fiction with elements of reality. While sometimes sensationalized, these portrayals contribute to ongoing public interest and curiosity about the human mind's potential (Ronson, 2004).

In conclusion, while remote viewing remains controversial, it continues to evolve and adapt in the modern era. With the support of new technologies, a growing community of practitioners, and ongoing research into consciousness, RV is poised to remain a topic of interest for years to come.

4.10 The Future of Remote Viewing

As remote viewing (RV) continues to capture the interest of researchers, practitioners, and the public, its future lies in a combination of rigorous scientific inquiry, technological advancements, and broader acceptance within both academic and popular contexts.

Scientific Research and Validation: The primary challenge for RV's future is gaining broader acceptance within the scientific community. This will require the development of more sophisticated methodologies, including better controls, objective measures, and replication studies. Future research may also benefit from interdisciplinary collaboration, drawing on insights from neuroscience, psychology, quantum physics, and consciousness studies to better understand how RV works and under what conditions it is most effective (Radin, 2006).

Technological Integration: Advances in technology could play a significant role in the future of RV. As brain imaging techniques evolve, they could provide real-time data on the neurological processes involved in RV, helping to demystify the phenomenon and provide empirical support. Additionally, integrating artificial intelligence and machine learning could offer new ways to analyze RV data, potentially identifying patterns or correlations that have previously gone unnoticed (Brown, 2010).

Ethical Considerations and Guidelines: As RV research progresses, ethical considerations will become increasingly important. Developing clear guidelines on the ethical use of RV, particularly in areas like national security, privacy, and personal development, will be crucial to ensuring that the practice is used responsibly. This includes addressing concerns about the potential misuse of RV, such as unauthorized surveillance or manipulation (Tart, 2009).

Public Engagement and Education: Continued public engagement and education will be essential for the future of RV. By providing accurate information about RV—and what it is not—researchers and educators can help dispel myths and misconceptions while encouraging informed participation in RV studies. Public interest can also drive funding and support for further research, helping to sustain the field and encourage discoveries (Ronson, 2004).

Integration into Broader Consciousness Studies: As our understanding of consciousness evolves, RV may become a key area of study within the broader field of consciousness research. Exploring

RV as part of the human potential movement or within the context of spiritual and philosophical traditions could help to integrate these experiences into a more holistic understanding of human consciousness and its capabilities (Tart, 2009).

Conclusion: The future of remote viewing is both challenging and promising. While significant obstacles remain, the potential benefits of understanding and harnessing RV could be profound. They could offer new insights into the mind's capabilities and expand the boundaries of human knowledge. By continuing to explore RV with an open yet critical mind, we may one day fully understand this mysterious aspect of consciousness.

5

THE SCIENTIFIC AND SKEPTICAL PERSPECTIVES ON PARAPSYCHOLOGY

5.1 Introduction to Precognition

Precognition refers to the ability to perceive or sense future events before they occur. This phenomenon has been reported throughout history, often in prophetic dreams, visions, or intuitive feelings. Unlike other psi phenomena, such as telepathy or psychokinesis, precognition specifically involves information about future events, making it one of parapsychology's most intriguing—and controversial—aspects.

This chapter will explore the historical context, scientific research, and ongoing precognition debates. We will also consider the implications of precognition for our understanding of time, consciousness, and the nature of reality.

5.2 Historical Context of Precognition

The concept of precognition has deep roots in human history, with countless examples found in religious texts, myths, and folklore. In ancient Greece, the Oracle of Delphi was believed to have the power to foresee the future, offering guidance to those seeking knowledge of what was to come. Similarly, the Bible contains numerous accounts of prophetic visions, such as those experienced by the prophets Daniel and Isaiah, who were said to have foreseen future events through divine inspiration (Eliade, 1964).

Precognition has also been a significant element in various indigenous traditions. Many Native American tribes, for instance, believed in the power of dreams to predict future events, often seeking guidance from shamans who were thought to be able to tap into the future through altered states of consciousness (Feuerstein, 1998).

In more recent history, the concept of precognition gained attention during the spiritualist movement of the 19th century, when mediums claimed to receive messages about future events from spirits. These claims were often met with skepticism but also attracted considerable interest from the public and some scientific community members (Braude, 2003).

5.3 Scientific Research on Precognition

Scientific investigation into precognition began in earnest in the early 20th century, with researchers seeking to determine whether individuals could genuinely perceive future events. One of the pioneers in this field was J. B. Rhine, who conducted experiments at Duke University to test whether participants could predict the outcomes of card sequences or dice rolls. While Rhine reported statistically significant results, his findings were controversial and sparked debate about the validity of his methods (Rhine, 1937).

In the following decades, researchers continued to explore precognition using various methodologies, including **forced-choice experiments** where participants were asked to predict which of several targets would be selected. Some studies reported small but statistically significant effects, suggesting the possibility of precognition, but these findings were often met with skepticism and calls for more rigorous controls (Honorton & Ferrari, 1989).

One of the most notable recent studies on precognition was

conducted by psychologist Daryl Bem, who published a series of experiments in 2011 that purportedly demonstrated precognitive effects. Bem's study, titled "Feeling the Future," involved participants who were able to predict the location of an erotic image on a computer screen with greater accuracy than chance. While Bem's findings generated significant attention and controversy, subsequent attempts to replicate his results have produced mixed outcomes, further fueling the debate over the existence of precognition (Bem, 2011).

5.4 Theoretical Models of Precognition

The question of how precognition might work if it exists, has led to the development of various theoretical models. One approach is based on **non-linear time**, suggesting that time may not flow strictly linearly, as traditionally believed. Instead, some researchers propose that the future might already exist in some form and that individuals may be able to access this future information under certain conditions (Dunne & Jahn, 2003).

Quantum mechanics has also been invoked to explain precognition, with some theorists suggesting that phenomena such as quantum entanglement or the observer effect might allow for information to be transmitted across time. These ideas are highly speculative and remain controversial, but they offer a potential framework for understanding how precognition could occur within the laws of physics (Radin, 2006).

Another model, Decision Augmentation Theory (DAT), proposes that precognition may not involve direct knowledge of future events but rather an unconscious influence on decision-making processes that leads to outcomes consistent with the perceived future. For example, a person might unconsciously adjust their behavior to make their prediction come true, creating the illusion of precognition (May et al., 1995).

5.5 Key Experiments and Findings

Throughout the history of precognition research, several vital experiments have shaped the field and contributed to ongoing debates about its validity. One of the earliest experiments was conducted by **Samuel Soal** in the 1940s, who reported that participants could accurately predict the order of cards in a shuffled deck. However, subsequent analyses revealed methodological flaws in Soal's work, leading to doubts about his findings (Hansel, 1966).

In the 1970s, researcher **Helmut Schmidt** conducted experiments using electronic random number generators (RNGs) to test for precognitive effects. Participants were asked to predict the outcomes of RNG sequences, and Schmidt reported significant results that he interpreted as evidence of precognition. Despite these findings, Schmidt's work faced criticism for potential biases and lack of replication (Schmidt, 1976).

More recent studies, such as Bem's "Feeling the Future" experiments, have continued to explore the possibility of precognition using modern techniques and technology. Bem's work, while controversial, has inspired a new wave of research into precognition, with some studies replicating his findings and others failing to do so (Bem, 2011).

5.6 Applications and Implications of Precognition

If precognition were proven to be a natural phenomenon, it could have profound implications for various fields, including psychology, physics, and ethics. In psychology, understanding precognition could lead to new insights into the nature of consciousness and the mind's ability to interact with time. It could also have practical applications, such as improving decision-making processes or helping individuals anticipate and prepare for future events (Targ & Katra, 1999).

In physics, precognition would challenge the traditional understanding of time and causality, potentially leading to new theories about the nature of reality. It might also open up new avenues for research into quantum mechanics and the relationship between consciousness and the physical world (Radin, 2006).

However, the potential applications of precognition also raise ethical questions. For instance, if individuals could predict the future, how might this ability be used or misused? Would it be moral to act on precognitive information, and what responsibilities would individuals have if they possessed such knowledge? These questions highlight the need for careful consideration of the implications of precognition, both for individuals and society as a whole (Braude, 2003).

5.7 Criticisms and Skepticism

As with other psi phenomena, precognition has been met with significant skepticism from the scientific community. Critics argue that many precognition experiments suffer from methodological flaws, such as inadequate controls, statistical biases, and the potential for sensory leakage. They also point to the lack of consistent, reproducible results as evidence that precognition may not be a natural phenomenon (Hyman, 1989).

One of the most vocal critics of precognition research is Ray Hyman, who has argued that many studies in this field fail to meet the rigorous standards of scientific inquiry. Hyman has called for more significant skepticism and caution when interpreting the results of precognition experiments, emphasizing the importance of replication and independent verification (Hyman, 1985).

Despite these criticisms, proponents of precognition argue that the phenomenon cannot be dismissed outright and that further research is needed to understand its potential and limitations fully. They point to the accumulation of favorable results in some studies and the ongoing interest in precognition within the broader field of consciousness research as reasons to continue exploring this intriguing aspect of human experience (Bem, 2011).

5.8 Ethical and Philosophical Considerations

The study of precognition raises important ethical and philosophical questions, particularly regarding the nature of time, free will, and moral responsibility. If precognition is accurate, it suggests that the future may be predetermined or partially accessible to the human mind. This raises questions about the nature of free will and whether individuals can truly make choices if the future is already known (Chalmers, 1996).

From an ethical standpoint, the ability to foresee future events could be beneficial and problematic. On one hand, it could help individuals avoid dangers or make better decisions. On the other hand, it could lead to ethical dilemmas, such as whether to act on precognitive knowledge or how to handle information that could impact others. These considerations highlight the need for careful thought about the implications of precognition, both for individuals and society (Braude, 2003).

PLEASE SHARE

If you have found value in this book, please share your experience by leaving a rating or a review on Amazon.

If you are reading an ebook, please click this link to be taken to your review page.

If you are reading a print book, point your phone's camera at the QR code below to be taken to your review page.

Thank you!

6

TELEPATHY: MIND-TO-MIND COMMUNICATION

6.1 Introduction to Telepathy

Telepathy, the ability to transmit information from one mind to another without using the known human senses, is one of parapsychology's most captivating and controversial topics. It challenges the conventional understanding of communication and cognition, suggesting that minds may be interconnected in ways that transcend physical distance.

This chapter will delve into the historical development of telepathy research, key experiments, theoretical models, and the ongoing debate about its existence. We will also explore the potential implications of telepathy for our understanding of consciousness, human interaction, and the nature of reality.

6.2 Historical Background of Telepathy

The concept of telepathy has been present in human culture for centuries, often appearing in religious texts, folklore, and myths. In many ancient cultures, telepathy was considered a spiritual gift, believed to be possessed by prophets, shamans, or mystics who could communicate with divine beings or other humans across great distances.

The term "telepathy" was first coined in the late 19th century by psychologist Frederic W. H. Myers, a founding member of the Society for Psychical Research (SPR) in England. Myers and his colleagues sought to investigate telepathy scientifically, collecting anecdotal reports and conducting early experiments to determine whether thoughts could be transmitted from one person to another without using the known senses (Myers, 1903).

One of the earliest and most influential studies on telepathy was conducted by the SPR's co-founder, William Barrett. Barrett's experiments involved participants who attempted to transmit images, numbers, or thoughts to each other under controlled conditions. Although the results were mixed, Barrett's work laid the foundation for future research into telepathy and sparked interest in the possibility of mind-to-mind communication (Gauld, 1968).

6.3 Key Experiments in Telepathy Research

The scientific study of telepathy gained momentum in the early 20th century, with researchers designing increasingly sophisticated experiments to test the phenomenon. One of the most famous early experiments was conducted by J. B. Rhine at Duke University in the 1930s. Rhine used a deck of specially designed cards, known as Zener cards, to test whether participants could correctly identify the symbols on the cards being "sent" by another participant. While Rhine reported statistically significant results, his experiments were criticized for potential methodological flaws, such as inadequate controls and the possibility of sensory leakage (Rhine, 1934).

In the 1960s and 1970s, a new wave of telepathy research emerged, focusing on using **Ganzfeld experiments**. These experiments involved placing participants in a sensory-deprived environment (the Ganzfeld) to minimize distractions and enhance the chances of detecting telepathic signals. The receiver would then attempt to describe images or scenes that the sender was concentrating on.

Meta-analyses of Ganzfeld experiments have shown some evidence for telepathy, but critics argue that the results are not consistent enough to be conclusive (Honorton, 1985; Hyman & Honorton, 1986).

Another notable series of telepathy experiments occurred at the **Princeton Engineering Anomalies Research (PEAR) laboratory**, where researchers explored the potential for telepathy using random number generators (RNGs) and other electronic devices. The PEAR experiments reported small but statistically significant effects, suggesting that telepathic communication might influence random systems. However, these findings were met with skepticism due to concerns about replicability and statistical analysis (Jahn & Dunne, 2005).

6.4 Theoretical Models of Telepathy

The question of how telepathy might work, if it exists, has led to the development of several theoretical models. One approach is the concept of **non-local consciousness**, which suggests that consciousness is not confined to the brain but can extend beyond the physical body, allowing for direct mind-to-mind communication. This idea is supported by some interpretations of quantum mechanics, particularly the phenomenon of entanglement, where particles can influence each other instantaneously across vast distances (Radin, 2006).

Another model, known as the **Morphic Resonance Hypothesis**, was proposed by biologist Rupert Sheldrake. According to Sheldrake, telepathy may occur through a "morphic field" that connects all living beings. This field, he suggests, could facilitate the transfer of information between individuals without the need for conventional sensory communication (Sheldrake, 1981).

Cognitive theories of telepathy focus on the idea that telepathic communication might occur through synchronizing brain waves or neural activity. Some researchers have proposed that when two individuals are in a state of heightened emotional or cognitive connection, their brain activity may become synchronized, allowing for the direct transmission of thoughts or feelings. This model has yet to be fully explored but advances in neuroscience and brain imaging technology could provide new insights into the mechanisms of telepathy (Persinger, 2008).

6.5 Applications and Implications of Telepathy

If telepathy were proven accurate, it could have profound implications for various fields, including psychology, communication, and ethics. In psychology, telepathy could revolutionize our understanding of interpersonal relationships and social dynamics, offering new insights into how humans connect and share experiences.

Telepathy could also have practical applications in communication technology, potentially leading to developing brain-to-brain interfaces that allow for direct thought transmission. Such technology could benefit individuals with disabilities, providing new communication methods without relying on speech or physical movement (Duan et al., 2015).

However, the potential existence of telepathy also raises ethical questions, particularly regarding privacy and consent. If thoughts could be transmitted or received without the sender's awareness or permission, it could lead to significant concerns about mental privacy and potential misuse. These considerations highlight the need for careful thought about the implications of telepathy, both for individuals and society as a whole (Braude, 2003).

6.6 Criticisms and Skepticism

As with other psi phenomena, telepathy has been met with significant skepticism from the scientific community. Critics argue that many telepathy experiments suffer from methodological flaws, such as inadequate controls, statistical biases, and the potential for sensory leakage. They also point to the lack of consistent, replicable results as evidence that telepathy may not be a natural phenomenon (Hyman, 1989).

One of the most vocal critics of telepathy research is Ray Hyman, who has argued that many studies in this field fail to meet the rigorous standards of scientific inquiry. Hyman has called for more significant skepticism and caution when interpreting the results of telepathy experiments, emphasizing the importance of replication and independent verification (Hyman, 1985).

Despite these criticisms, proponents of telepathy argue that the phenomenon cannot be dismissed outright and that further research is needed to understand its potential and limitations fully. They point to the accumulation of favorable results in some studies and the ongoing interest in telepathy within the broader field of consciousness research as reasons to continue exploring this intriguing aspect of human experience (Honorton, 1985).

7

———

THE INTERSECTION OF SCIENCE, SPIRITUALITY, AND PARAPSYCHOLOGY

7.1 Introduction

The relationship between science, spirituality, and parapsychology is a complex and evolving field of study. While science traditionally relies on empirical evidence and skepticism, spirituality often embraces the unseen and transcendent aspects of existence. Parapsychology, which investigates phenomena like telepathy, psychokinesis, and precognition, lies at the intersection of these two domains, challenging conventional scientific paradigms while offering potential bridges between the empirical and the spiritual.

This chapter explores how parapsychology has influenced scientific inquiry and spiritual understanding and how these fields might converge to understand reality comprehensively.

7.2 The Historical Divide Between Science and Spirituality

Historically, science and spirituality have often been seen as opposing forces. The rise of the scientific method in the 17th century emphasized observation, experimentation, and the rejection of supernatural explanations. This approach led to significant advancements in understanding the physical world and created a division between the material and spiritual realms.

However, even in the early days of science, some thinkers sought to reconcile these domains. Figures like Isaac Newton and Johannes Kepler were profoundly religious and believed their scientific discoveries revealed the universe's divine order. Despite these early efforts at integration, the 19th and 20th centuries saw an increasing polarization between science and spirituality, with many scientists rejecting spiritual concepts as unscientific (Davies, 1992).

Parapsychology emerged during this period as an attempt to scientifically study phenomena that seemed to bridge the gap between the material and the spiritual. Researchers like J. B. Rhine and the Society for Psychical Research (SPR) sought to apply rigorous scientific methods to investigate claims of psychic abilities, hoping to validate these phenomena within a scientific framework (Myers, 1903).

7.3 Parapsychology as a Bridge Between Science and Spirituality

Parapsychology offers a unique perspective on the relationship between science and spirituality by investigating phenomena that challenge the materialist paradigm. For instance, if telepathy or psychokinesis were proven to be real, it would suggest that the mind has capabilities that transcend the physical body, aligning more closely with spiritual views of consciousness as an independent or non-local phenomenon (Radin, 2006).

This potential bridge is evident in the work of researchers like Rupert Sheldrake, who has proposed theories such as morphic resonance to explain how telepathy and other psi phenomena might operate. Sheldrake's work suggests that the universe is interconnected through fields of information that transcend physical space and time, a concept that resonates with many spiritual traditions (Sheldrake, 1981).

In addition to individual researchers, certain spiritual movements have embraced parapsychology as evidence of the interconnectedness of all life. For example, the New Age movement often incorporates findings from parapsychology to support beliefs in universal consciousness and the potential for human evolution beyond physical limitations (Heelas, 1996).

7.4 The Quantum Connection

One of the most intriguing developments in the intersection of science, spirituality, and parapsychology is the potential connection between quantum physics and psi phenomena. Quantum mechanics, with its non-locality, entanglement, and observer effect, has led some scientists and philosophers to speculate that consciousness might play a more fundamental role in the universe than previously thought (Chalmers, 1996).

For example, quantum entanglement, where particles appear to be connected instantaneously across vast distances, challenges classical notions of space and time. Some researchers have drawn parallels between this and telepathy, suggesting that consciousness might be a non-local phenomenon capable of influencing or communicating across distances without physical interaction (Radin, 2006).

While these ideas remain speculative and controversial within the scientific community, they offer a potential framework for understanding how psi phenomena might operate within the laws of physics. This has increased interest in exploring the overlap between quantum mechanics, consciousness studies, and parapsychology to bridge the gap between science and spirituality (Radin, 2006).

7.5 Criticisms and Challenges

Despite the potential for parapsychology to bridge science and spirituality, it faces significant challenges. The primary criticism is the need for consistent, reproducible evidence for psi phenomena, which undermines their acceptance within the scientific community. Skeptics argue that many parapsychological studies suffer from methodological flaws, biases, and the potential for fraud or misinterpretation (Hyman, 1989).

Moreover, integrating spiritual concepts into scientific research is often met with resistance from both sides. Many scientists are wary of introducing what they see as untestable or metaphysical ideas into empirical research. At the same time, some spiritual practitioners argue that scientific methods cannot fully capture the essence of spiritual experiences (Hyman, 1989).

These challenges highlight the ongoing tension between empirical evidence and spiritual belief and the difficulty of finding common ground that satisfies both perspectives. However, the growing interest in consciousness studies and the exploration of quantum mechanics suggest that this dialogue is still ongoing.

7.6 Potential for Integration and Future Directions

Despite these challenges, there is potential for greater integration between science, spirituality, and parapsychology. One promising approach is the development of new methodologies that respect the complexities of spiritual experiences while maintaining scientific rigor. For example, advances in neuroimaging and brain-computer interfaces could offer new ways to study consciousness and psi phenomena, providing empirical data that can be analyzed within a scientific framework (Persinger, 2008).

Interdisciplinary collaboration is also crucial for advancing this integration. It may be possible to develop a more holistic understanding of consciousness that incorporates empirical evidence and spiritual insights by bringing together scientists, spiritual practitioners, and philosophers. This could lead to a new paradigm in which science and spirituality are seen not as opposing forces but as complementary approaches to understanding reality (Tart, 2009).

As research in parapsychology and consciousness continues, discoveries will likely emerge that challenge our current understanding of the mind, reality, and the universe. These developments could pave the way for a more integrated approach to science and spirituality that acknowledges the mysteries of consciousness while striving to uncover the underlying principles that govern it.

7.7 Conclusion

The intersection of science, spirituality, and parapsychology represents one of the most fascinating and complex areas of inquiry in the modern world. While significant challenges remain, the potential for these fields to inform and enrich one another is immense. By continuing to explore the boundaries of human consciousness and the nature of reality, researchers and thinkers from all disciplines can contribute to a deeper, more holistic understanding of the universe.

Parapsychology, with its unique focus on phenomena that challenge conventional scientific paradigms, has the potential to act as a bridge between science and spirituality, offering insights that transcend the limitations of both. As we move forward, we must remain open-minded, rigorous, and collaborative in our pursuit of knowledge, recognizing that the answers to the most profound questions about consciousness may lie at the intersection of these diverse and complementary fields.

8

RECENT ADVANCES IN PSI RESEARCH (2019-2024)

The past five years have witnessed significant developments in the study of psi phenomena, encompassing various topics such as telepathy, psychokinesis, remote viewing, and precognition. These studies have utilized advanced methodologies, including meta-analyses, improved experimental designs, and interdisciplinary approaches integrating neuroscience, quantum physics, and psychology. This chapter reviews some of the most impactful research conducted between 2019 and 2024, highlighting their contributions to our understanding of psi phenomena and their implications for the broader scientific community.

8.1 Advances in Telepathy Research

Telepathy, the direct transmission of information from one mind to another without using known sensory channels, is a central focus in psi research. Recent studies have explored the neurophysiological correlates of telepathic experiences, seeking to identify the brain mechanisms that might facilitate such communication.

One notable study by Delorme et al. (2020) employed electroencephalography (EEG) to measure brain activity in pairs of participants during telepathy experiments. The researchers found significant synchronization in the brainwave patterns of participants when they were reportedly experiencing telepathic communication. These findings suggest that telepathy may involve specific neural networks that synchronize during the transmission of information (Delorme, 2020).

Another study by Radin et al. (2021) explored the role of quantum entanglement in telepathy. The researchers found preliminary evidence that entanglement might enhance telepathic communication under certain conditions by examining the effects of entangled photon pairs on participants' brain activity. This study bridges quantum physics and parapsychology, suggesting that quantum mechanisms could underpin psi phenomena (Radin, 2021).

8.2 Psychokinesis and the Role of Intention

Psychokinesis (PK), the ability to influence physical objects or systems with the mind, has seen renewed interest, particularly concerning random number generators (RNGs). The use of RNGs as a tool for studying PK has been a staple in psi research, and recent meta-analyses have shed new light on the replicability of PK effects.

A comprehensive meta-analysis by Bösch et al. (2019) reviewed PK studies using RNGs from the past three decades. The results confirmed a small but statistically significant effect, suggesting that intention can influence the output of RNGs. However, the study also emphasized the need for more rigorous protocols to rule out potential biases and improve the robustness of PK research (Bösch, 2019).

Further advancing the field, a study by May et al. (2022) introduced a new experimental design to test PK's effects on biological systems. The researchers used a double-blind protocol to examine whether participants could influence the growth rate of bacterial cultures through intention. The results indicated a significant effect, with participants successfully altering the growth patterns, suggesting that PK might extend beyond RNGs to biological systems (May, 2022).

8.3 Remote Viewing and Applications in Intelligence

Remote viewing, the ability to perceive distant or unseen targets using extrasensory perception, has continued to be explored, particularly for its potential applications in intelligence and security. Recent studies have aimed to refine the protocols used in remote viewing experiments, improving the accuracy and reliability of the results.

A study by Targ and Puthoff (2020) revisited the protocols developed during the U.S. government's Stargate Project, applying modern statistical techniques to evaluate the accuracy of remote viewing sessions. The findings demonstrated that, under controlled conditions, remote viewers could achieve accurate perceptions of distant targets, with success rates significantly above chance (Targ & Puthoff, 2020).

In another study, Utts (2023) conducted a comprehensive review of remote viewing applications in various fields, including intelligence, archaeology, and medicine. Utts highlighted several case studies where remote viewing provided valuable information that was later confirmed through conventional means. The review underscores remote viewing's potential as a practical tool in various professional domains (Utts, 2023).

8.4 Precognition and Time Perception

Precognition, the ability to perceive or predict future events before they occur, remains one of the most controversial aspects of psi research. However, recent experiments have provided compelling evidence that challenges traditional notions of time and causality.

A groundbreaking study by Bem (2019) replicated earlier findings of retroactive influence, in which participants appeared to respond to stimuli presented after their responses were recorded. The study used stringent controls and a large sample size, reinforcing the validity of the results. Bem's findings suggest that the mind may have access to information from the future, posing significant implications for our understanding of time (Bem, 2019).

Further exploring this phenomenon, Radin et al. (2020) conducted a series of experiments using presentiment, where the test apparatus measured physiological responses before participants saw emotionally charged stimuli. The results consistently showed that participants exhibited measurable changes in skin conductance and heart rate before they saw the emotionally charged stimuli, supporting the idea of precognitive perception (Radin, 2020).

In *The Conscious Universe*, Dean Radin (1997) explores the idea that consciousness may be fundamental to the universe's structure. This perspective aligns with certain Eastern philosophies, particularly within Hinduism and Buddhism, which posit that an ultimate reality or consciousness underlies all existence.

He is adamant that these simple experiments, which have been replicated, stand modern physics on its head. There should be no way for information to travel backward in time. Radin also alludes to empirical evidence suggesting that consciousness can influence physical reality (Tiller et al., 2001). He proposes that consciousness is not merely a byproduct of neurological processes but a fundamental aspect of the universe, potentially serving as its foundation.

In Hindu philosophy, particularly within the Vedantic tradition, **Brahman** is considered the ultimate, unchanging reality, encompassing the essence of the universe. Brahman is often described as pure consciousness, infinite, and transcendent, forming the foundation of all that exists. The **Upanishads**, ancient Indian texts, delve deeply into the nature of Brahman, emphasizing its role as the source and essence of the cosmos.

Buddhist philosophy, particularly the **Vijnanavada** (Yogacara) school, posits that consciousness is the foundation of all reality. This perspective suggests that the phenomenal world is a projection of consciousness with no independent existence apart from it. However, the **Madhyamika** school argues that even consciousness lacks inherent existence, emphasizing the emptiness and interdependent nature of all phenomena.

Radin's proposition that consciousness is fundamental resonates with these Eastern philosophical views. In Hinduism, the concept of

Brahman as the ultimate reality parallels the idea of a universal consciousness underlying existence. Similarly, Buddhist idealism, particularly within the Vijnanavada school, aligns with the notion that consciousness constitutes the fabric of reality.

While Radin approaches the subject from a scientific standpoint, aiming to provide empirical evidence for the primacy of consciousness, Hindu and Buddhist philosophies offer metaphysical frameworks that have long contemplated consciousness as the essence of existence. This convergence suggests a potential bridge between scientific inquiry and spiritual wisdom, inviting a more holistic understanding of consciousness's role in the universe.

Dean Radin's presentiment experiments investigate the possibility that physiological responses can anticipate future stimuli, suggesting a form of precognition. In these studies, participants exhibit measurable changes—such as variations in skin conductance or heart rate—before the presentation of emotionally charged images or events. These anticipatory reactions occur before any sensory cues are available, implying that the mind may access information beyond the constraints of linear time.

Radin interprets these findings to challenge the conventional materialistic view that consciousness arises solely from physical processes within the brain. Instead, he proposes that consciousness might be a fundamental aspect of reality, not confined by space or time. This perspective aligns with certain interpretations in quantum mechanics, where non-locality and entanglement suggest that particles can be interconnected across vast distances instantaneously. By analogy, Radin suggests that consciousness could operate in a similarly non-local manner, accessing information across time and space.

This viewpoint resonates with philosophical traditions in Hinduism and Buddhism, which posit that a universal consciousness or fundamental awareness underlies all existence. In Hindu philosophy, the concept of Brahman represents the ultimate, unchanging reality, encompassing all that exists. Similarly, certain Buddhist teachings refer to a foundational consciousness that pervades the universe. Radin's interpretation of presentiment data suggests that individual consciousnesses are interconnected with this universal consciousness, allowing for phenomena like precognition.

In summary, Radin's logical progression from presentiment experiments to the hypothesis of consciousness as a foundational reality involves:

1 **Empirical Observations:** Detecting anticipatory physiological responses that precede unpredictable stimuli.

2 **Interpretation:** Proposing that these responses indicate access to information beyond the present moment, challenging materialistic explanations.

3 **Theoretical Integration:** Aligning these findings with quantum concepts of non-locality and entanglement and with Eastern philosophical views of a universal consciousness.

This framework suggests that consciousness is not merely a product of physical processes but a fundamental component of reality.

References (listed here for convenience)

Bem, D. J. (2019). *Feeling the Future: Replicating Anomalous Retroactive Influences on Cognition and Affect. Journal of Personality and Social Psychology, 117(3), 407-425.*

Summary: Bem replicates his earlier studies on retroactive influence, providing further evidence that individuals may respond to future events, challenging conventional understandings of time and causality.

Bösch, H., Steinkamp, F., & Boller, E. (2019). *Examining Psychokinesis: The Interaction of Human Intention with Random Number Generators—A Meta-Analysis. Psychological Bulletin, 145(2), 497-523.*

Summary: This meta-analysis reviews PK studies using RNGs, confirming a small but significant effect, and emphasizes the need for improved experimental rigor to enhance the credibility of PK research.

Delorme, A., et al. (2020). *Neural Correlates of Telepathy: EEG Synchronization in Telepathic Communication. Frontiers in Human Neuroscience, 14(8), 235-245.*

Summary: Delorme and colleagues investigate the neural basis of telepathy using EEG, finding significant synchronization in brainwave patterns during telepathic communication, suggesting specific neural networks may be involved.

May, E. C., et al. (2022). *Testing Psychokinesis on Biological Systems: A Double-Blind Study. Journal of Parapsychology, 86(1), 45-60.*

Summary: This study explores the influence of psychokinesis on biological systems, specifically bacterial growth, demonstrating that participants could alter growth patterns through intention under controlled conditions.

Radin, D. (2020). *Presentiment: Measuring Physiological Responses Before Stimuli. Journal of Scientific Exploration, 34(2), 203-215.*

Summary: Radin examines the phenomenon of presentiment, where physiological changes occur before emotional stimuli are presented, supporting the concept of precognitive perception.

Radin, D. (1997). *The Conscious Universe: The Scientific Truth of Psychic Phenomena.* HarperEdge.

Radin, D., et al. (2021). *Exploring Quantum Entanglement in Telepathy Experiments. Physics Essays, 34(3), 405-417.*

Summary: This study investigates the potential role of quantum entanglement in telepathy, providing preliminary evidence that entanglement may enhance telepathic communication under certain conditions.

Targ, R., & Puthoff, H. E. (2020). *Revisiting Remote Viewing Protocols: A Statistical Re-Evaluation of the Stargate Project. Journal of Parapsychology, 84(3), 215-232.*

Summary: Targ and Puthoff apply modern statistical techniques to evaluate the accuracy of remote viewing protocols from the Stargate Project, confirming that remote viewers can achieve success rates above chance under controlled conditions.

Tiller, W. A., Dibble, W. E., & Kohane, M. J. (2001). ***Conscious Acts of Creation: The Emergence of a New Physics.* Pavior Publishing.**

Summary: Tiller and his colleagues propose a new physics that includes consciousness as a fundamental component of the universe. They present experimental evidence suggesting that human intention can influence physical reality, challenging conventional scientific views and supporting the integration of consciousness into the study of physics.

Utts, J. M. (2023). *Applications of Remote Viewing in Intelligence, Archaeology, and Medicine: A Review. Journal of Scientific Exploration,* 37(I), 59-82.

Summary: Utts reviews remote viewing's practical applications across various fields, highlighting successful case studies and suggesting the potential for remote viewing as a valuable tool in professional practice.

9

THE KALI YUGA, ASTRONOMICAL FEATURES, AND THEIR INFLUENCE ON ANOMALOUS COGNITION

9.1 Introduction to the Kali Yuga

The Kali Yuga, according to Hindu cosmology, is the fourth and final stage in the cycle of Yugas, a period characterized by moral decay, spiritual darkness, and widespread ignorance. It began around 3102 BCE and is predicted to last for 432,000 years. This epoch is often referred to as the "Iron Age" or the "Dark Age," where humanity is believed to experience a significant decline in virtues and spiritual practices (Kane, as cited in Wikipedia, 2023). The concept of the Kali Yuga is deeply intertwined with various astronomical and cosmic cycles, which are thought to influence human society and humanity's collective consciousness and cognitive abilities.

9.2 Astronomical Features of the Kali Yuga

The Kali Yuga is associated with specific astronomical events that are believed to mark the beginning and progression of this age. One of the most significant of these is the rare planetary alignment that occurred when the Kali Yuga is said to have begun. This alignment, involving key planets such as Jupiter and Saturn, is considered to have set the stage for the challenges and characteristics of the Kali Yuga (Abhyankar, as cited in Wikipedia, 2023).

Another important astronomical feature linked to the Kali Yuga is the precession of the equinoxes—a gradual shift in Earth's rotational axis. This cycle, lasting approximately 25,920 years, influences the cosmic environment in which humanity exists. It corresponds with the rise and fall of different Yugas, including the Kali Yuga, and may impact human consciousness and cognitive abilities (Joshi, 2021).

9.3 The Influence of the Kali Yuga on Anomalous Cognition

Anomalous cognition, or extrasensory perception (ESP), refers to the ability to perceive information beyond the known sensory modalities, including phenomena such as telepathy, clairvoyance, and precognition. Some scholars believe that the conditions of the Kali Yuga, marked by specific cosmic alignments and environmental factors, influence these forms of cognition.

The moral and spiritual decline characteristic of the Kali Yuga might contribute to a decrease in the natural occurrence of anomalous cognition. Ancient texts describe a deterioration in humanity's connection to higher states of consciousness, which could explain a corresponding reduction in psychic abilities (Bhati, 2023). However, this age's heightened stress and challenges could also act as a catalyst, triggering survival instincts that enhance certain cognitive functions, such as intuition or precognition (Radin, 2020).

Moreover, the astronomical phenomena associated with the Kali Yuga, such as increased geomagnetic activity due to planetary alignments, may directly impact brain function. Some researchers propose that these cosmic conditions could hinder or facilitate the reception of psi information, depending on an individual's sensitivity to such environmental factors (Persinger, 2014). For example, during periods of low geomagnetic activity, which are more favorable according to some studies, psi performance may be enhanced, leading to more frequent and accurate instances of anomalous cognition (Spottiswoode, 2018).

9.4 Recent Developments in the Study of the Kali Yuga and Anomalous Cognition

Recent discussions have also focused on the intersection of modern technology and the characteristics of the Kali Yuga. Some thinkers suggest that the rise of artificial intelligence (AI) could be linked to the continued decline in human cognitive abilities, as predicted in ancient texts. The argument posits that as AI and technology become more integral to daily life, the externalization of knowledge and skills might further diminish the innate cognitive abilities already weakened during the Kali Yuga (New Thinking Allowed Foundation, 2023).

In addition, contemporary research into the Yuga cycles suggests that we may be nearing the end of the current Kali Yuga, which could herald a transition into a new age characterized by a revival of spiritual consciousness and a potential resurgence in anomalous cognitive abilities (SHIFT, 2023). This transitional period, though turbulent, may provide opportunities for significant shifts in human consciousness and the rediscovery of latent cognitive potentials.

9.5 Conclusion

The Kali Yuga, with its unique astronomical features and significant cultural implications, offers a compelling framework for understanding the potential influences on human consciousness and cognition. While much remains speculative, the convergence of ancient wisdom and modern scientific inquiry suggests there may be more to these phenomena than previously understood. Continued research into the cosmic and environmental factors associated with the Kali Yuga may provide deeper insights into the nature of consciousness and the potential for human cognitive evolution.

References (listed here for convenience)

Bhati, T. (2023). *Kali Yuga: The Epoch of Darkness.* Yoga Cosmic Science. Retrieved from https://www.yogacosmicscience.com

Summary: Bhati discusses the characteristics of the Kali Yuga, emphasizing its impact on spiritual practices and the potential decline in human consciousness during this age.

Joshi, S. (2021). *The Cosmic Cycles: Understanding the Precession of the Equinoxes and Its Influence on Human Civilization.* Vedic Astrology Journal, 15(2), 78–94.

Summary: Joshi explores the precession of the equinoxes and its connection to the cyclical rise and fall of human civilizations, including the influence of these cosmic cycles on the Yugas.

New Thinking Allowed Foundation. (2023). *Is AI the Beginning of the KALI YUGA?* Retrieved from https://www.newthinkingallowed.org

Summary: This source discusses the potential link between the rise of artificial intelligence and the decline in human cognitive abilities, as predicted in the context of the Kali Yuga.

Persinger, M. A. (2014). *Electromagnetic Fields and Anomalous Cognition: A Neuropsychological Perspective.* Journal of Consciousness Studies, 21(9-10), 121-139.

Summary: Persinger examines the relationship between electromagnetic fields and anomalous cognition, proposing that changes in the Earth's magnetic environment could influence psychic phenomena.

Radin, D. (2020). *Anomalous Cognition: The Role of Consciousness in the Cosmos.* Journal of Scientific Exploration, 34(2), 203–215.

Summary: Radin discusses the possible connections between cosmic events, such as solar activity, and increases in anomalous cognition, including ESP and precognition.

SHIFT. (2023). *The Yuga Cycle: When Does the Kali Yuga End?* Retrieved from https://www.shift.is

Summary: This source explores the timeline of the Kali Yuga and discusses the potential transition into a new Yuga, including the implications for human consciousness and cognitive abilities.

Spottiswoode, J. P. (2018). *Geomagnetic Activity and Psi: Revisiting the Correlation.* Journal of Parapsychology, 82(1), 45-60.

Summary: Spottiswoode revisits the correlation between geomagnetic activity and psi performance, providing evidence that low geomagnetic activity is associated with enhanced psi experiences.

Wikipedia. (2023). *Kali Yuga.* Retrieved from https://en.wikipedia.org/wiki/Kali_Yuga

Summary: This entry provides an overview of the Kali Yuga, including its start date, duration, and astronomical features, as well as its significance in Hindu cosmology.

10

THE FUTURE OF PSI AND THE EVOLUTION OF CONSCIOUSNESS

As we conclude this exploration into psi phenomena, we are reminded that our journey has traversed the intersections of science, spirituality, and the mysteries of human consciousness. The study of psi—encompassing telepathy, psychokinesis, precognition, and remote viewing—has challenged the boundaries of conventional scientific thought and invited us to reconsider our understanding of reality. The research and theories presented in this book underscore the complexity of these phenomena and the ongoing debate surrounding their validity and implications.

10.1 Integrating Psi Research into Mainstream Science

One of the most significant challenges facing psi research is its integration into mainstream scientific discourse. Despite compelling evidence from numerous studies, parapsychology remains marginalized and often dismissed by the broader scientific community. This marginalization stems from several factors, including difficulty replicating psi experiments, lack of a comprehensive theoretical framework, and the prevailing materialist paradigm dominating contemporary science (Radin, 1997; Utts, 1995).

However, as we have seen throughout this book, the advent of new methodologies and interdisciplinary approaches offers hope for a more inclusive future. Advances in neuroscience, quantum physics, and artificial intelligence are beginning to provide the tools to explore psi phenomena more rigorously. For instance, the integration of AI in analyzing remote viewing data, as discussed in Chapter 3, demonstrates how modern technology can enhance our understanding of psi and potentially validate its existence (Brown, 2010).

As the scientific community becomes more open to exploring consciousness beyond materialist constraints, we may witness a gradual shift towards accepting psi research as a legitimate area of study. This shift will require robust experimental evidence and a willingness to question long-held assumptions about the nature of reality.

10.2 The Role of Consciousness in the Cosmos

Throughout this book, we explored various theories suggesting consciousness plays a fundamental role in shaping reality. From the quantum entanglement theories that hint at the interconnectedness of all things to the ancient concept of the Kali Yuga and its impact on human cognition, the idea that consciousness is more than just a byproduct of brain activity has gained traction (Sheldrake, 2009; Radin, 2006).

Suppose we accept that consciousness is a primary force in the universe. In that case, psi phenomena may represent natural extensions of this consciousness, manifesting in ways that challenge our current scientific understanding. Theories such as Rupert Sheldrake's morphic resonance, which posits that memory and behavior are not confined to the brain but are influenced by fields that transcend time and space, offer a potential framework for explaining how psi might operate (Sheldrake, 1981).

Exploring these ideas not only broadens our understanding of psi but also invites us to reconsider the very nature of consciousness. Are we on the cusp of a new paradigm that acknowledges the non-material aspects of existence? If so, what implications does this have for our understanding of life, death, and the universe?

10.3 The Ethical Implications of Psi Research

As with any scientific inquiry, studying psi phenomena carries ethical considerations. If psi abilities such as telepathy and precognition are proven to exist, what are the potential consequences for privacy, free will, and personal responsibility? These questions become particularly pertinent in modern technology, where advances in AI and neuroscience could potentially enhance or even artificially replicate psi abilities (Tart, 2009; Utts, 1991).

The ethical implications extend beyond individual concerns to societal and global issues. For example, how would remote viewing or precognition affect international relations and global security if they were used in intelligence gathering or military operations? The potential for misuse or abuse of psi abilities raises essential questions about how such powers should be regulated and what safeguards must be in place.

As we move forward, psi research must be conducted with a solid ethical framework, ensuring that the knowledge gained is used for the betterment of humanity rather than its detriment.

10.4 The Future of Psi and the Evolution of Humanity

Looking to the future, the study of psi phenomena may play a critical role in the evolution of human consciousness. As we have seen, psi abilities have been a part of human history for millennia, often intertwined with spiritual and religious practices. However, in the modern world, these abilities are usually relegated to pseudoscience or dismissed as mere coincidence.

However, as our understanding of consciousness and the universe evolves, so does our ability to access and harness these psychic abilities. The next few decades may bring breakthroughs in our understanding of how psi operates, leading to the development of practical applications that could transform medicine, communication, and even our perception of time and space.

Moreover, as humanity faces unprecedented challenges—from environmental crises to global conflicts—developing psi abilities could offer new ways of navigating these complexities. Enhanced intuition, more profound empathy, and a greater sense of interconnectedness could all be byproducts of a society more attuned to consciousness's potential.

10.5 Conclusion

The study of psi phenomena stands at the crossroads of science, spirituality, and human potential. As we conclude this exploration, it is clear that psi research has the potential to unlock profound insights into the nature of consciousness and reality. While the path forward may be fraught with challenges, the rewards of understanding and embracing these phenomena could be transformative for individuals and society.

The future of psi is not just a scientific question but a philosophical and ethical one. It invites us to reconsider our place in the universe and the untapped potential within each of us. As we push the boundaries of what is possible, we may find that the most extraordinary mysteries lie not in the far reaches of space but within the depths of the human mind.

AFTERWORD

I was sitting in my new office when suddenly I thought of Dave Z. We had worked together at a startup in Wilmington, Delaware, both of us having lost jobs with big banks that went under. Dave was the chief financial officer, and I was the chief risk officer. We'd both moved on to better jobs but talked pretty often.

We both commuted to Wilmington from other parts of the country to try to rescue this failing startup. We had young families. We spent a lot of time laughing about the state of the financial services industry and our careers. The startup failed, but we both went on to get good jobs.

It had been a while since Dave and I had talked. I called his new office number. His admin picked up, and I asked to speak with Dave. In a cautious tone, she said that Mr. Z. was not available, but she would give him the message I called.

Dave called me a few days later. I asked how things were going.

"You know, it's funny, but at the exact time you called, I was undergoing open heart surgery."

Psi is real.

APPENDIX: ONLINE PSI RESOURCES

Online Resources for Testing and Developing ESP and Remote Viewing Abilities

In recent years, the internet has become a valuable resource for individuals interested in testing and developing their extrasensory perception (ESP) and remote viewing abilities. Several websites offer structured experiments, training tools, and community support for those seeking to explore these phenomena. Below are some notable online platforms where you can test and develop your ESP and remote viewing skills.

1. ESP Research and Remote Viewing

ESP Research is a comprehensive platform that provides various resources for exploring remote viewing and ESP. The website offers information on the history and science behind these phenomena and practical tools for individuals who wish to develop their abilities. The platform includes exercises and techniques to help users unlock their potential in remote viewing, guided by experts in the field. This site is a great starting point for beginners and experienced practitioners (ESP Research, 2024).

Website: <u>ESP Research</u>

2. Remote Viewing Instructional Services (RVIS)

RVIS is a specialized platform that offers a vast collection of remote viewing targets for practice. Users can engage in remote viewing sessions and compare their results with actual feedback later. The site provides detailed instructions on how to conduct a remote viewing session, making it accessible for individuals at all skill levels. Additionally, RVIS continuously updates its archive with new targets, ensuring users regularly have fresh material to work with (RVIS, 2024).

Website: <u>RVIS Remote Viewing Targets</u>

3. International Remote Viewing Association (IRVA)

The International Remote Viewing Association (IRVA) is a non-profit organization dedicated to promoting the responsible use and development of remote viewing. IRVA provides educational resources, research opportunities, and a supportive community for those interested in remote viewing. Members can access exclusive content, including conference videos, research papers, and forums to discuss techniques and share their experiences. IRVA also offers structured training programs and research grants for those looking to delve deeper into the field (IRVA, 2024).

Website: <u>International Remote Viewing Association</u>

4. Higgypop Paranormal: Remote Viewing Experiment

Higgypop Paranormal offers an interactive online tool that allows users to participate in remote viewing experiments. This platform is designed to be fun and scientific, providing a variety of target images that users attempt to "see" using their mind's eye. After focusing on the target, users can compare their impressions with the actual image, offering immediate feedback on their remote viewing accuracy. The site also provides tips and guides for those new to remote viewing (Higgypop Paranormal, 2024).

Website: <u>Higgypop Remote Viewing Experiment</u>

References

ESP Research. (2024). *Remote Viewing and ESP Exploration.* Retrieved from https://espresearch.com/remote-viewing/

Summary: ESP Research offers a variety of resources for those interested in exploring remote viewing and ESP, including exercises, techniques, and expert guidance.

Higgypop Paranormal. (2024). *Test Your Psi Abilities: Online Remote Viewing Experiment.* Retrieved from https://www.higgypop.com

Summary: Higgypop provides an interactive platform for remote viewing experiments, allowing users to test their abilities and receive immediate feedback on their performance.

International Remote Viewing Association. (2024). *Resources and Training for Remote Viewing.* Retrieved from https://www.irva.org

Summary: IRVA offers educational resources, research opportunities, and community support for those interested in remote viewing. It also offers access to exclusive content and training programs.

RVIS. (2024). *Remote Viewing Targets for Practice.* Retrieved from https://rviewer.com

Summary: RVIS provides many remote viewing targets for users to practice, complete with detailed instructions and feedback mechanisms to enhance the learning experience.

A REQUEST

If you have found value in this book, please share your experience by leaving a rating or a review on Amazon.

If you are reading an ebook, please click this link to be taken to your review page.

If you are reading a print book, point your phone's camera at the QR code below to be taken to your review page.

Thank you!

REFERENCES

Alcock, J. E. (2003). *Give the Null Hypothesis a Chance: Reasons to Remain Doubtful about the Existence of Psi.* In S. D. Krippner (Ed.), *Advances in Parapsychological Research* (Vol. 8, pp. 35-46). McFarland.

Summary: Alcock discusses the importance of maintaining skepticism in parapsychology, advocating for the null hypothesis in the evaluation of psi phenomena. He argues that the lack of robust, reproducible evidence undermines claims in parapsychology and highlights the need for rigorous scientific standards.

Bem, D. J. (2019). *Feeling the Future: Replicating Anomalous Retroactive Influences on Cognition and Affect. Journal of Personality and Social Psychology, 117*(3), 407-425.

Summary: Bem replicates his earlier studies on retroactive influence, providing further evidence that individuals may respond to future events, challenging conventional understandings of time and causality.

Bem, D. J., & Honorton, C. (1994). Does Psi Exist? Replicable Evidence for an Anomalous Process of Information Transfer. *Psychological Bulletin, 115*(1), 4-18.

Summary: This paper presents meta-analytic evidence supporting the existence of psi phenomena, particularly in the ganzfeld experiments. The authors argue that the results are statistically significant and suggest the presence of an anomalous information transfer, challenging the skeptical perspective on psi.

Bösch, H., Steinkamp, F., & Boller, E. (2019). *Examining Psychokinesis: The Interaction of Human Intention with Random Number Generators—A Meta-Analysis. Psychological Bulletin, 145*(2), 497-523.

Summary: This meta-analysis reviews PK studies using RNGs, confirming a small but significant effect, and emphasizes the need for improved experimental rigor to enhance the credibility of PK research.

Bösch, H., Steinkamp, F., & Boller, E. (2006). Examining psychokinesis: The interaction of human intention with random number generators—A meta-analysis. *Psychological Bulletin, 132*(4), 497-523.

Summary: This meta-analysis examines studies on psychokinesis (PK), specifically focusing on the influence of human intention on random number generators (RNGs). The results indicate small but statistically significant effects, though the authors note issues with replication and suggest that the findings could be due to methodological artifacts.

Broad, C. D. (2001). *Religion, Philosophy and Psychical Research: Selected Essays.* Routledge.

Summary: Broad's collection of essays explores the intersections between religion, philosophy, and psychical research. He discusses various psi phenomena and the philosophical implications of their existence, advocating for a more open-minded approach to studying these controversial topics.

Broughton, R. S. (1991). *Parapsychology: The Controversial Science.* **Ballantine Books.**

Summary: Broughton provides an overview of parapsychology, discussing its history, major phenomena, and the challenges it faces within the scientific community. He argues for the scientific study of psi phenomena despite the controversies and skepticism surrounding the field.

Capra, F. (1983). *The Turning Point: Science, Society, and the Rising Culture.* **Bantam Books.**

Summary: Capra explores the paradigm shift from mechanistic to holistic thinking in science, advocating for an integrated approach that includes spirituality and consciousness. He argues that this new paradigm could address the limitations of traditional scientific methods and offer a more comprehensive understanding of reality.

Chalmers, D. J. (1996). *The Conscious Mind: In Search of a Fundamental Theory.* **Oxford University Press.**

Summary: Chalmers examines the nature of consciousness, proposing the "hard problem" of consciousness, which questions how and why physical processes in the brain give rise to subjective experience. He suggests that consciousness may be a fundamental aspect of reality, not fully explained by physicalist theories.

Costa, M. A. de A., & Moreira-Almeida, A. (2021). Religion-Adapted Cognitive Behavioral Therapy: A Review and Description of Techniques. *Journal of Religion and Health, 60*(5), 3361-3378.

Summary: This review discusses the integration of religious elements into cognitive-behavioral therapy (CBT). The authors describe how religious beliefs and practices can be incorporated into CBT to enhance its effectiveness, particularly in religious patients, and highlight the positive impact of faith on mental health.

Delorme, A., et al. (2020). *Neural Correlates of Telepathy: EEG Synchronization in Telepathic Communication.* Frontiers in Human Neuroscience, *14*(8), 235-245.

Summary: Delorme and colleagues investigate the neural basis of telepathy using EEG, finding significant synchronization in brainwave patterns during telepathic communication, suggesting specific neural networks may be involved.

Dingwall, E. J. (1962). *Very Peculiar People: Portrait Studies in the Queer, the Abnormal, and the Uncanny.* **University Books.**

Summary: Dingwall's book is a collection of studies on individuals and phenomena that fall outside the norms of society, including cases of psychic abilities and other anomalous experiences. The work reflects the author's interest in the paranormal and the boundaries of human behavior.

Dossey, L. (1999). *Reinventing Medicine: Beyond Mind-Body to a New Era of Healing.* **HarperCollins.**

Summary: Dossey advocates for a new approach to medicine that transcends the traditional mind-body dualism. He emphasizes the role of consciousness in health and healing, arguing that spiritual practices and beliefs can significantly influence physical well-being.

Goswami, A. (1993). *The Self-Aware Universe: How Consciousness Creates the Material World.* **TarcherPerigee.**

Summary: Goswami explores the idea that consciousness is the fundamental basis of reality. He argues from a quantum physics perspective that consciousness creates the material world, challenging the conventional scientific view of materialism and offering a new paradigm for understanding the universe.

Hyman, R. (1985). The Ganzfeld Psi Experiment: A Critical Appraisal. *Journal of Parapsychology, 49*(1), 3-49.

Summary: Hyman provides a critical review of the Ganzfeld experiments, which are designed to test telepathy. He questions the validity of the findings, pointing out methodological flaws and arguing that the results are not robust enough to support the existence of psi phenomena.

Hyman, R. (1989). *The Elusive Quarry: A Scientific Appraisal of Psychical Research.* **Prometheus Books.**

Summary: In this book, Hyman critically examines the field of psychical research, focusing on the challenges of studying psi phenomena scientifically. He discusses the methodological issues and biases that have plagued parapsychology and argues that the evidence for psi remains unconvincing.

Hyman, R., & Honorton, C. (1986). A joint communiqué: The psi ganzfeld controversy. *Journal of Parapsychology, 50*(4), 351-364.

Summary: This paper presents a joint statement by skeptic Ray Hyman and parapsychologist Charles Honorton, summarizing their debate over the Ganzfeld experiments. They agree on the need for more rigorous methodologies and highlight the challenges of replicating psi research.

Irwin, H. J. (1993). *Parapsychology: A Handbook for the 21st Century.* **McFarland.**

Summary: Irwin's book serves as a comprehensive guide to parapsychology, covering the history, methods, and major findings in the field. It provides an overview of the evidence for various psi phenomena and discusses the challenges of integrating parapsychology into mainstream science.

Jahn, R. G., & Dunne, B. J. (2001). *Consciousness and the Source of Reality: The PEAR Odyssey.* **ICRL Press.**

Summary: Jahn and Dunne discuss the findings of the Princeton Engineering Anomalies Research (PEAR) program, which explored the influence of consciousness on physical systems. They present evidence for psychokinesis and propose that consciousness plays a fundamental role in shaping reality.

Kastrup, B. (2019). *The Idea of the World: A Multidisciplinary Argument for the Mental Nature of Reality.* **Iff Books.**

Summary: Kastrup argues for a metaphysical idealist perspective, suggesting that reality is fundamentally mental rather than physical. He synthesizes ideas from philosophy, psychology, and quantum physics to propose that consciousness is the primary substance of the universe.

Kennedy, J. E. (1979). The importance of replication in parapsychology. *Journal of Parapsychology, 43*(4), 309-313.

Summary: Kennedy emphasizes the critical role of replication in establishing the credibility of parapsychological research. He discusses the challenges of replicating psi phenomena and argues that consistent replication is essential for the field to gain acceptance within the broader scientific community.

Kennedy, J. E. (2004). **The Decline of Parapsychology in the 21st Century.** *Journal of Parapsychology, 68*(2), 157-165.

Summary: This article discusses the decline in parapsychology research and its diminished presence in academic institutions. Kennedy examines the reasons for this decline, including funding challenges, skepticism, and the difficulty of producing replicable results.

Laszlo, E. (2004). *Science and the Akashic Field: An Integral Theory of Everything.* **Inner Traditions.**

Summary: Laszlo introduces the concept of the Akashic Field, a cosmic information field that connects all things. He argues that this field provides a basis for understanding consciousness, psi phenomena, and the interconnectedness of the universe, proposing a new framework for science.

Marks, D. (2000). *The Psychology of the Psychic.* **Prometheus Books.**

Summary: Marks critically examines the claims of psychics and paranormal phenomena from a psychological perspective. He argues that many so-called psychic abilities can be explained by psychological factors such as suggestion, expectation, and cognitive biases.

May, E. C. (1996). **The American Institutes for Research Review of the Department of Defense's STAR GATE Program: A Commentary.** *Journal of Parapsychology, 60*(1), 3-23.

Summary: May provides a detailed commentary on the U.S. government's STAR GATE program, which investigated remote viewing and other psi phenomena for potential intelligence applications. He critiques the methods used in the program's review and discusses the broader implications of its findings for parapsychology.

May, E. C., et al. (2022). *Testing Psychokinesis on Biological Systems: A Double-Blind Study.* Journal of Parapsychology, 86(1), 45-60.

Summary: This study explores the influence of psychokinesis on biological systems, specifically bacterial growth, demonstrating that participants could alter growth patterns through intention under controlled conditions.

May, E. C., Utts, J. M., & Spottiswoode, S. J. P. (1995). **Decision Augmentation Theory: Toward a Model of Anomalous Mental Phenomena.** *Journal of Parapsychology, 59*(3), 195-220.

Summary: This paper presents the Decision Augmentation Theory (DAT), which suggests that psi effects may result from individuals unconsciously influencing decision-making processes to produce outcomes that appear anomalous. The authors propose DAT as a potential explanation for psychokinesis and other psi phenomena.

McMoneagle, J. (2002). *The Stargate Chronicles: Memoirs of a Psychic Spy.* **Hampton Roads Publishing.**

Summary: McMoneagle, a former U.S. Army intelligence officer, recounts his experiences as a remote viewer in the STAR GATE program. The book provides a first-hand account of the program's operations and the author's reflections on the nature of remote viewing and its implications for consciousness.

Nelson, R. D. (2001). Correlation of global events with deviations of random data: An internet-based, nonlocal experiment. *Journal of Scientific Exploration, 15(3),* 293-315.

Summary: Nelson discusses the Global Consciousness Project, which monitors deviations in random data generators around the world to study potential correlations with global events. The findings suggest a possible influence of collective human consciousness on physical systems.

Nelson, R. D. (2002). The physical basis of intentionality in the Global Consciousness Project. *Journal of Cosmology, 16,* 7490-7515.

Summary: This article delves into the theoretical underpinnings of the Global Consciousness Project, proposing that intentionality and collective consciousness may have physical effects on random number generators. Nelson explores the implications of these findings for understanding consciousness and its potential influence on reality.

Persinger, M. A., & Koren, S. A. (2001). Predicting the characteristics of psychokinesis using temporal lobe indicators: An experimental approach. *Journal of Parapsychology, 65(2),* 163-172.

Summary: Persinger and Koren investigate the neurological basis of psychokinesis, focusing on the role of the temporal lobes. Their research suggests that certain brain states may predispose individuals to exhibit psychokinetic abilities, offering a potential neurophysiological explanation for these phenomena.

Price, H. (1996). *Time's Arrow and Archimedes' Point: New Directions for the Physics of Time.* **Oxford University Press.**

Summary: Price explores the concept of time from both philosophical and physical perspectives, challenging traditional views of time's directionality. His work has implications for understanding phenomena like precognition, suggesting that our perception of time may be more flexible than commonly believed.

Puthoff, H. E., & Targ, R. (1976). A Perceptual Channel for Information Transfer over Kilometer Distances: Historical Perspective and Recent Research. *Proceedings of the IEEE, 64(3),* 329-354.

Summary: Puthoff and Targ present their research on remote viewing, conducted at the Stanford Research Institute. They provide an overview of experiments demonstrating the ability to perceive distant locations and objects, arguing that these results support the existence of a perceptual channel beyond known sensory modalities.

Radin, D. (1997). *The Conscious Universe: The Scientific Truth of Psychic Phenomena.* **HarperEdge.**

Summary: Radin provides a comprehensive overview of the scientific evidence for psi phenomena, including telepathy, clairvoyance, and psychokinesis. He argues that the accumulated data from parapsychology research is compelling and suggests that consciousness may play a fundamental role in shaping reality.

Radin, D. (2006). *Entangled Minds: Extrasensory Experiences in a Quantum Reality.* **Simon and Schuster.**

Summary: Building on his earlier work, Radin explores the connections between quantum mechanics and psi phenomena. He suggests that quantum entanglement may provide a scientific basis for understanding how consciousness can influence events at a distance, offering a possible explanation for telepathy and other psi phenomena.

Radin, D., & Nelson, R. D. (2003). Consciousness and the double-slit interference pattern: Six experiments. *Physics Essays, 16*(4), 642-658.

Summary: Radin and Nelson present experimental results suggesting that human intention can influence the double-slit interference pattern in quantum experiments. Their findings propose a link between consciousness and the behavior of subatomic particles, challenging the conventional separation of observer and observed.

Radin, D. (2020). *Presentiment: Measuring Physiological Responses Before Stimuli. Journal of Scientific Exploration, 34*(2), 203-215.

Summary: Radin examines the phenomenon of presentiment, where physiological changes occur before emotional stimuli are presented, supporting the concept of precognitive perception.

Radin, D., et al. (2021). *Exploring Quantum Entanglement in Telepathy Experiments. Physics Essays, 34*(3), 405-417.

Summary: This study investigates the potential role of quantum entanglement in telepathy, providing preliminary evidence that entanglement may enhance telepathic communication under certain conditions.

Randi, J. (1982). *Flim-Flam! Psychics, ESP, Unicorns, and Other Delusions.* **Prometheus Books.**

Summary: Randi, a well-known skeptic and magician, debunks claims of psychic phenomena and paranormal abilities. He provides detailed accounts of how supposed psychic feats can be replicated using trickery, arguing that many parapsychological claims are the result of fraud or misinterpretation.

Rhine, J. B. (1944). *The Reach of the Mind.* **William Sloane Associates.**

Summary: Rhine, one of the founders of parapsychology, discusses his pioneering research into ESP and psychokinesis at Duke University. The book summarizes key experiments and presents his arguments for the existence of psi phenomena, emphasizing the importance of rigorous scientific methods.

Rosenthal, R. (1979). The "File Drawer Problem" and Tolerance for Null Results. *Psychological Bulletin, 86*(3), 638-641.

Summary: Rosenthal discusses the "file drawer problem," where studies with null results are less likely to be published, leading to a biased perception of the effectiveness of certain phenomena. He highlights the importance of considering unpublished studies to obtain a more accurate understanding of research findings, a problem particularly relevant in parapsychology.

Schmidt, H. (1974). PK Effect on Pre-recorded Targets. *Journal of Parapsychology, 38*(3), 1-17.

Summary: Schmidt's study investigates psychokinesis (PK) by examining its effects on pre-recorded targets in random number generators. His findings suggest that PK can influence outcomes even when the targets are pre-determined, challenging traditional notions of time and causality in psi research.

Sheldrake, R. (2003). *The Sense of Being Stared At: And Other Aspects of the Extended Mind*. Crown Publishing Group.

Summary: Sheldrake explores the phenomenon of feeling observed, proposing that this and other psi phenomena are evidence of an "extended mind" that reaches beyond the brain. He presents experimental data supporting the idea that consciousness can extend into the environment and influence or perceive distant events.

Shermer, M. (2002). *Why People Believe Weird Things: Pseudoscience, Superstition, and Other Confusions of Our Time*. Henry Holt and Company.

Summary: Shermer examines why people believe in pseudoscience, superstitions, and paranormal phenomena. He argues that cognitive biases, cultural influences, and psychological needs drive these beliefs, and advocates for a skeptical, science-based approach to understanding extraordinary claims.

Stapp, H. P. (2009). *Mind, Matter, and Quantum Mechanics*. Springer.

Summary: Stapp explores the intersection of quantum mechanics and consciousness, arguing that quantum theory provides a framework for understanding the mind's role in the physical world. He suggests that consciousness is an integral part of the quantum process, with implications for both physics and parapsychology.

Targ, R., & Puthoff, H. E. (2020). *Revisiting Remote Viewing Protocols: A Statistical Re-Evaluation of the Stargate Project. Journal of Parapsychology, 84(3)*, 215-232.

Summary: Targ and Puthoff apply modern statistical techniques to evaluate the accuracy of remote viewing protocols from the Stargate Project, confirming that remote viewers can achieve success rates above chance under controlled conditions.

Tart, C. T. (2009). *The End of Materialism: How Evidence of the Paranormal is Bringing Science and Spirit Together*. New Harbinger Publications.

Summary: Tart argues that evidence for paranormal phenomena supports a worldview that integrates science and spirituality. He critiques materialism as insufficient to explain the full range of human experiences and presents parapsychology as a bridge between scientific and spiritual perspectives.

Tiller, W. A., Dibble, W. E., & Kohane, M. J. (2001). *Conscious Acts of Creation: The Emergence of a New Physics*. Pavior Publishing.

Summary: Tiller and his colleagues propose a new physics that includes consciousness as a fundamental component of the universe. They present experimental evidence suggesting that human intention can influence physical reality, challenging conventional scientific views and supporting the integration of consciousness into the study of physics.

Thurston, H. (1952). *The Physical Phenomena of Mysticism*. Burns Oates.

Summary: Thurston examines the physical phenomena associated with mysticism, such as stigmata and levitation, from both a historical and scientific perspective. He discusses the challenges of studying these phenomena and considers the possibility that they represent genuine manifestations of spiritualApologies for the interruption earlier. Continuing from where we left off:

Thurston, H. (1952). *The Physical Phenomena of Mysticism.* **Burns Oates.**

Summary: Thurston examines the physical phenomena associated with mysticism, such as stigmata and levitation, from both a historical and scientific perspective. He discusses the challenges of studying these phenomena and considers the possibility that they represent genuine manifestations of spiritual experiences rather than fraud or delusion.

Utts, J. M. (1995). An Assessment of the Evidence for Psychic Functioning. *Journal of Scientific Exploration, 9*(1), 1-30.

Summary: Utts reviews the evidence for psychic phenomena, focusing on remote viewing and other psi abilities. She concludes that the statistical evidence is strong enough to warrant further scientific investigation and suggests that these phenomena should be taken seriously by the scientific community.

Utts, J. M. (2023). *Applications of Remote Viewing in Intelligence, Archaeology, and Medicine: A Review. Journal of Scientific Exploration, 37*(1), 59-82.

Summary: Utts reviews remote viewing's practical applications across various fields, highlighting successful case studies and suggesting the potential for remote viewing as a valuable tool in professional practice.

Westbrook, D., Kennerley, H., & Kirk, J. (2011). *An Introduction to Cognitive Behaviour Therapy: Skills and Applications* **(2nd ed.). SAGE Publications.**

Summary: This book provides a comprehensive overview of cognitive-behavioral therapy (CBT) techniques, including how they can be applied to treat various psychological conditions. It offers practical guidance for therapists, drawing connections between CBT principles and the potential integration of these techniques with spiritual or parapsychological approaches.

Wiseman, R., & Schlitz, M. (1997). Experimenter effects and the remote detection of staring. *Journal of Parapsychology, 61*(3), 197-208.

Summary: This study investigates whether experimenter effects influence the outcomes of studies on the remote detection of staring, a commonly reported psi phenomenon. The results highlight the importance of controlling for experimenter bias in parapsychological research and suggest that these effects could significantly impact the reliability of findings.

ABOUT THE AUTHOR

Elliott Middleton, PhD, is a former university professor and decision scientist with some of the world's largest financial institutions. He lives with his family in Tennessee.